Forward by Josh Peck

HIGHER DIMENSIONS
Parallel Dimensions & the Spirit Realm

Daniel Duval

Higher Dimensions, Parallel Dimensions

&

The Spirit Realm

by Daniel Duval

Bride Publications

Copyright © 2016 by Daniel Duval

Unless otherwise noted, all Scripture quotations are taken from the King James Version of the Bible.

Scripture quotations marked (AMPC) are taken from the Amplified Bible, Classic Edition, Copyright © 1954, 1958, 1962, 1964, 1965, 1987 by The Lockman Foundation. Used by permission.

Unless otherwise noted, all Hebrew and Greek words were taken from www.blueletterbible.org.

Cover Design by Gonz Shimura http://www.facelikethesun.com.

Please make any requests to use or reprint material from this book to Daniel Duval through the contact page on www.bridemovement.com.

ISBN: 978-1-94384-459-3 (Print)
ISBN: 978-1-94384-498-2 (ebook)

DEDICATION

This book is dedicated to the forerunners in the body of Christ. It is dedicated to those who refuse to settle and to those who choose to overcome against all odds. It is dedicated to those that choose to go the distance with God and who refuse to be intimidated by the unknown. This book is also dedicated to the survivors that I work with, who are some of the bravest people on the planet.

TABLE OF CONTENTS

Foreword

I have a deep passion for quantum physics. I have an even deeper passion for the truth contained in the Bible. I have dedicated much of my time and effort trying to show how the two are not only comparable, but compatible. One of the biggest blessings I have come across in my ministry is the fact that I am not alone in this pursuit; there are other researchers who share my passion in their own unique way.

Dan Duval is absolutely one of these people. He, like me, puts the truth of the word of God first and foremost, but also shows that science can aide in the pursuit of truth. Dan does this with an incredibly unique perspective. He applies the understanding of quantum physics to spiritual warfare, prophecy, and what we have to look forward to as believers in Jesus Christ.

The first time I ever spoke with Dan, I honestly didn't know what to think. We, along with two others, were guests on *Opposing the Matrix*, hosted by my personal friend, Jim Wilhelmsen. At the time, I was researching for my book *Quantum Creation* and unbeknownst to me, Dan was involved in similar research. For a researcher/author, there is a short pang of panic whenever we hear another is currently looking into the same subjects we are preparing to write about. No one wants to step on anyone's toes and we all want to offer information in our own unique way. Throughout the show we spoke about our respective works. Over time, it became more and more apparent that, while our research had a certain element of overlap, we were both coming from unique perspectives.

Now, I probably should explain my comment about "not knowing what to think" of Dan initially. When I was listening to Dan speak, it was absolutely clear that he knew what he was talking about. However, prior to this show, I was not familiar with Dan Duval or his ministry. On the show, he was speaking with the confidence and authority of a seasoned researcher and author. I was not expecting this. I hoped this confidence was coming from a place of experience and a genuine desire to help people in spiritual need. However, shameful as it is for me to admit, a piece of me feared it may have been coming from a place of pride. Today, I am blessed to proclaim that my fear was absolutely, undeniably, and unequivocally false.

After the show, I had a couple of opportunities to talk to Dan one-on-one. We later met in person at a prophecy conference we were both invited to. Before that time, I had never met an individual with his level of confidence who had managed to remain humble. However, upon getting to know Dan personally, and especially meeting him in person, I realized he is everything a good servant of the Lord should be. I detected not an ounce of pride in him. What I did detect was an extremely intelligent individual with an impressive amount of confidence and charisma, yet with a servant's heart filled with humility, meekness, and love. This is an extremely rare combination that, at least for me, is a breath of fresh air in a broken world.

After the conference, Dan and I stayed in touch. He was kind enough to invite me on his radio show and we had some excellent conversations. I was thrilled, not only to speak to an honest researcher, but to speak with someone who had no problem keeping up with my off-the-wall and fringe ideas. Many times throughout the shows I forgot I was on the radio, and felt as though I was just in a conversation with a good friend.

It is a rare thing to come across an individual with a way of making you feel like a better person just for knowing him. That's Dan Duval. Not only can one learn a great deal of head-knowledge from Dan's research, ministry, and outreach, but one can learn a great a deal of heart-knowledge as well. In my personal reading of *Higher Dimensions, Parallel Dimensions, & the Spirit Realm*, it is quite obvious to me that there is no one better qualified to write this book than Dan Duval. What you hold in your hands will not only equip you with vital information about science and the Bible, but will also serve as a look into a great man of God and his ministry; one that everyone willing can benefit from. A big and very special thanks goes out to Dan Duval for all of his hard work in serving the people God has called him to, for being a living example of the things Jesus has called us to be, and for the honor of his friendship.

Enjoy the book, take care, and God bless!

Josh Peck

www.ministudyministry.com

Introduction

What is a higher dimension? What is a parallel dimension? Do they exist? If so, what might one expect to find if we could, as they say, cross over to the other side? Would one find a copy of him or herself in a parallel dimension? Do parallel dimensions contain alternate timelines? Is there more than one earth? Where is God? In an ever-advancing world, many of these questions are now being asked. Judging by the fact that you picked up this book, you are likely the very one asking these questions.

There are many related subjects that warrant consideration. For instance, are there people in other dimensions? Are there aliens? Can angels operate in more than one dimension? Do they? What about sleep paralysis? Why does that happen to so many people? Are portals real? From a biblical perspective, does the atonement of Jesus apply to all dimensions or only the one in which we live?

Whether you're willing to admit it or not, you've probably pondered these questions at least a couple of times in your life. If nothing else, you may have gotten a headache and gone about your typical business, discarding the thoughts. But what would you do if you picked up a book that just so happened to claim that many of these questions could be answered? Would you have the audacity to read it?

Think about the implications of realizing that you exist on more than one dimensional plane. How might that change your life? Consider the intrigue of learning how one partakes of God's divine nature. Understanding higher dimensions opens the door to the unseen realm. It also has the potential to take the Christian faith to a whole new level. Are you ready to go there?

Not only will this book disclose the reality of higher dimensions and parallel dimensions, but it will also bring the understanding of these places into a practical context. What do you have to lose? Join me on an adventure into the unknown realms of eternity. This may just be the most powerful, eye-opening book you have ever read.

CHAPTER 1

Higher Dimensions Revealed

In order to properly understand higher dimensions, we must first establish how the Bible refers to them. *In the Bible, heavenly places are elements of higher dimensions.* This revelation is absolutely central to this work. Once we define our terms, we quickly realize that higher dimensions are actually a biblical concept. Thousands of years before quantum physics, the Bible established the fact that higher dimensions exist. As a matter of fact, not only do they exist, but they have an incredible influence upon the world in which we live.

Christians have been interacting with higher dimensions since the inception of the early church. They may not have called it what it was, but they did it nonetheless. Let's consider the upper room incident. After Jesus ascended to heaven, the disciples went to the upper room in Jerusalem to tarry until the Holy Spirit came upon them (Acts 1:9–13). The Holy Spirit arrived on the day of Pentecost.

THE DAY OF PENTECOST

"And when the day of Pentecost had fully come, they were all assembled together in one place, when suddenly there came a sound from heaven like the rushing of a violent tempest blast, and it filled the whole house in which they were sitting. And there appeared to them tongues resembling fire, which were separated and distributed and which settled on each one of them" (Acts 2:1–3 AMPC).

This was not a natural experience. Tongues resembling fire do not walk the earth. They do not naturally occur in our three-dimensional world. Instead, these tongues resembling fire appeared to the disciples from another dimension. *The reason that they <u>must</u> have manifested from another dimension is <u>because</u> they do not naturally occur in our own.* This isn't a new concept for most people who have read the Bible. However, it may be a new way to think about it.

Understand that there are both natural things and supernatural things. Natural things occur as part of the normal course of events in our world. Supernatural things occur, *yet are not* part of the normal course of events in our world. Supernatural events are *above* natural events. In the example from the Book of Acts, the gust of wind may have been written off as a natural thing. However, when the source of the wind was revealed (the tongues resembling fire), the whole event became supernatural. Natural things are confined to the dimension in which we exist physically. Supernatural things manifest from dimensions higher than (and in some cases parallel to) the dimension in which we exist. Clearly, the early church was interacting with higher dimensions (since the early church was officially born on the day of Pentecost).

So, where did these tongues resembling fire come from? They manifested from a heavenly place. Understand that whatever is seen, perceived, or manifested must exist, even if it does not exist in this dimension. Dimensionality, in many ways, unlocks the mysteries of existence. How do we establish a foundation that will allow us to understand things from a dimensional perspective? I propose that the conversation begins with the creation of heaven and earth.

CHAPTER 2

Dimensions of Creation and the Spiritual Universe

There has been a question that has been overlooked, brushed aside, and willfully ignored for a long time. It is a question that has empowered skeptics and presented a real problem for apologists. It is a question that many lay evangelists have groaned over. It may be a question you have personally wrestled with. This question is properly stated as follows: In the creation week, how is it possible that God spoke light into creation on day one, and then created the sun, moon, and stars on day four? If the sun, moon, and stars did not exist on day one, where was the light coming from? Furthermore, how was there day and night?

"And God said, Let there be light: and **there was light**. And God saw the light, that it was good: and God divided the light from the darkness. And God called the light Day, and the darkness he called Night. And the evening and the morning were **the first day**" (Genesis 1:3–5).

"And God said, Let there be lights in the firmament of the heaven to divide the day from the night; and let them be for signs, and for seasons, and for days, and years: And let them be for lights in the firmament of the heaven to give light upon the earth: and it was so. And **God made two**

great lights; the greater light to rule the day, and the lesser light to rule the night: **he made the stars also**. And God set them in the firmament of the heaven to give light upon the earth, and to rule over the day and over the night, and to divide the light from the darkness: and God saw that it was good. And the evening and the morning were **the fourth day**" (Genesis 1:14–19).

WHAT IS GOING ON?

We are taught that day and night exist on the physical earth due to its revolution around the sun. Although I acknowledge that there are pockets of people who are now arguing a "flat earth" perspective (which is an entirely separate conversation), the majority of people today hold to a cosmology that portrays a spherical earth rotating around a physical sun. This is known as the heliocentric model. Hundreds of years ago it replaced geocentrism, which is the view that places earth at the actual "center" of the universe, about which every other celestial body rotates.

Interestingly enough, my next question applies to both the heliocentric model and geocentrism equally. The question is, how could there be light on day one if the sun, moon, and stars did not exist until day four? While some would like to say the stars (including the sun) were "actually" created on day one, and that they became visible to earth on day four, this is simply unacceptable. It is a feeble attempt to argue away the obvious. This is not what the text says, and skeptics that point out the lunacy of this rebuttal are justified in doing so. I believe there is a better and more accurate explanation. It simply requires that we bring a dimensional element to the discussion.

A Better Explanation

So what is this better explanation? *Plainly stated, I believe that while there are many higher dimensions, the three-dimensional world in which we live is actually set atop a spiritual template.* Think about setting out to build a tower. First the support beams must be set in place, then the rest of the tower can be built on top of it. In like manner, I believe that God created our universe in the spirit first. He used the first two days to put the proverbial support beams in place. On subsequent days of the creation week, he put the physical creation on top of it. The question is, what would lead me to suggest such a thing?

As I attempted to address the issue created by the first and fourth days of creation, I began a word study that transformed everything. It utterly revolutionized my understanding of Scripture. It led me to conclude that in the original language and word use, there is not a single element of the creation account, prior to the third day of creation, requiring a "physical" interpretation. Instead, I found that the language (prior to the third day) was actually describing a spiritual creation. The third day was the transition point where the language began to demand a physical interpretation.

As I demonstrate this, it will essentially prove that there is, in fact, a spiritual template underneath the physical creation. This will show that creation is layered, and ultimately intertwines with other dimensions of existence. It will also point to the idea that it was "designed" this way. This may seem slightly far-fetched, but I believe that if you track with me, everything will make sense. It will also serve as a foundation for understanding other elements of this book.

In the Beginning

Beginning in Genesis 1:1, we find that the Bible explains how creation came into existence. God created the heavens, and he created the earth. I believe this means he created all of the dimensions of existence in addition to a spiritual earth. I further believe that in doing this he also tied all of creation to the earth. Therefore, the heavens and earth are present at the outset of creation week.

"In the beginning God (prepared, formed, fashioned, and) created the heavens and the earth" (Genesis 1:1 AMPC).

Moving into the second verse of Genesis, we find that God is preparing to format the earth for the present creation. In this assessment, I am ignoring all arguments relating to the debate of young earth versus old earth. All I am concerned with is explaining the *nature* of what happened. I am setting out to show that creation was first spiritual and secondarily physical. Therefore, can every element of Genesis 1:2 be interpreted as being entirely spiritual?

"And the earth was without form, and void; and darkness was upon the face of the deep. And the Spirit of God moved upon the face of the waters" (Genesis 1:2).

The key Hebrew words in this passage are as follows. The word *earth* is translated from the Hebrew word *erets*. This word straightforwardly means "earth." However, since I am arguing that this was a spiritual earth, the proof isn't going to come from the name of the planet, but from the other elements in this passage. The next import phrase is *without form*, which is translated from the Hebrew word *tohu*. This word means "formless, confusion, unreality, emptiness, and chaos." Consider just how clear this is. Here we find that earth was in a state of unreality. It was defined as emptiness. In my opinion, this is because it was a spiritual template.

The next important word is *void*, which is translated from the Hebrew word *bohu*. This word means "emptiness, void or waste." Again, I believe the clear intent is to show just how empty the unreality of earth was. This takes us to the word translated *darkness*, which is the Hebrew word *chosek*. This word means "darkness," "obscurity," or "secret place." The most interesting thing about the word *darkness* is its application in other passages. It is repeatedly used in reference to spiritual (and not literal) darkness. I believe this is because it was a spiritual component of the spiritual template that pre-existed the physical creation.

"For thou art my lamp, O Lord: and the Lord will lighten my darkness [chosek]" (2 Samuel 22:29).

"If I wait, the grave is mine house: I have made my bed in the darkness [chosek]" (Job 17:13).

"He brought them out of darkness [chosek] and the shadow of death, and brake their bands in sunder" (Psalm 107:14).

The list of Scriptures that apply darkness, or *chosek,* to spiritual realities is extensive. This was a spiritual darkness that was present. The next key word that we find is the word *deep*, which is translated from the Hebrew word *tehowm*. This word means "deep" or "abyss." Other definitions include "primeval ocean" and "grave." How fascinating! This becomes a highly interesting word study as we work our way through Scripture. *Tehowm* is referred to as a person with a voice and hands. It is also the force by which God destroyed the earth in the days of Noah. The deep is first spiritual, although it has power in the physical realm.

"The mountains saw thee, and they trembled: the overflowing of the water passed by: the deep [tehowm] uttered his voice, and lifted up his hands on high" (Habakkuk 3:10).

"In the six hundredth year of Noah's life, in the second month, the seventeenth day of the month, the same day were all the fountains of the great deep [tehowm] broken up, and the windows of heaven were opened" (Genesis 7:11).

Next, we see the Spirit of the Lord hovering over the waters. The word translated *water* is *mayim.* This word straightforwardly means "water." Is this water physical or spiritual? From many Scriptures we learn that water is found in the spirit realm as well as in the natural realm. Therefore, we still have no conflict. These waters were spiritual. Remember, I am attempting to prove that every element of creation prior to the third day of creation occurred in the spirit. Where do we see that water can exist in the spirit? One example is that Jesus Christ is the Source of Living Water. This is spiritual water.

"For my people have committed two evils; they have forsaken me the fountain of living waters, and hewed them out cisterns, broken cisterns, that can hold no water" (Jeremiah 2:13).

"For the Lamb which is in the midst of the throne shall feed them, and shall lead them unto living fountains of waters: and God shall wipe away all tears from their eyes" (Revelation 7:17).

Thus, after studying the first two verses of Scripture, we learn the following:

1. God created the dimensions of the higher heavens.
2. God created a spiritual earth.

3. The Spirit of the Lord hovered over the spiritual earth as God was preparing to form it.

THE FIRST DAY

This takes us to the first day of creation, which we have already quoted. God said let there be light, and there was light. The word *light* is translated from the Hebrew word *'owr*. This is the same word we find in the following passages.

"Yea, the light ['owr] of the wicked shall be put out, and the spark of his fire shall not shine" (Job 18:5).
"He will deliver his soul from going into the pit, and his life shall see the light ['owr]" (Job 33:28).
"Who coverest thyself with light ['owr] as with a garment: who stretchest out the heavens like a curtain" (Psalm 104:2).

Note that all of these verses are dealing with spiritual light. God put spiritual light into creation on the first day. Furthermore, since God is Light, and everything that was made, was made through Jesus (John 1:1–3), it would not be much of a stretch to say that this light was God manifesting himself to the creation template. Isn't it interesting that it is spiritual light determining day and night on the first day?

THE SECOND DAY

"And God said, Let there be a firmament in the midst of the waters, and let it divide the waters from the waters. And God made the firmament, and divided the waters which were under the firmament from the waters which were above the firmament: and it was so. And God called the firmament Heaven. And the evening and the morning were the second day" (Genesis 1:6–8).

Next we encounter the second day of creation. During this event, we find God dividing the waters from the waters. God creates a firmament and puts waters above and waters below. The word *firmament* means "a space" or "gap." In other words, God used the spiritual waters to set boundaries on the universe. This firmament is the space between earth and the boundaries or edges of our universe (whatever those may be). The waters above became a boundary between our universe and the higher areas of the heavens. The waters below were left to be incorporated into the creation of the physical earth. They were gathered together to become the spiritual template for the physical water of the planet.

Then we see that God called the firmament heaven. This is the "heaven" that manifested as a spiritual template for what we now call "outer space." As I will repeat later on, I believe that this is part of what is called the "second heaven." Just like God first set the proverbial beams of earth before placing a physical creation on top of it, God set the proverbial beams of the cosmos before placing a physical creation on top of it. In short, this firmament became the spiritual template for the cosmos.

THE THIRD DAY

It is at the outset of the third day that we reach a transition point. On the third day, the nature of the creation account changes. In the beginning, as well as on the first and second days, I believe it is clear that the entire creation was occurring in the spirit realm. Once the spiritual template was created, God was then able to begin his work on the physical elements of the universe. The creation account seems to describe a spiritual creation that God established to ultimately serve as the template for the physical creation. I find it incredibly interesting that instead of beginning with the stars and planets, the first celestial body in our universe to receive a physical creation was the earth. This places the spiritual earth at the center of all activity that is intended to take place in this universe. (I will note that this does not have to mean that the physical earth is positioned at the physical center of the physical universe).

> And God said, Let the waters under the heaven be gathered together unto one place, and let the dry land appear: and it was so. And God called the dry land Earth; and the gathering together of the waters called he Seas: and God saw that it was good. And God said, Let the earth bring forth grass, the herb yielding seed, and the fruit tree yielding fruit after his kind, whose seed is in itself, upon the earth: and it was so. And the earth brought forth grass, and herb yielding seed after his kind, and the tree yielding fruit, whose seed was in itself, after his kind: and God saw that it was good. And the evening and the morning were the third day.
>
> (Genesis 1:9–13)

On the third day the waters under heaven were gathered together. They were gathered to one place which is earth. It was at this point that dry land appeared. "Dry land" indicates that God was putting the physical creation on top of the spiritual template. The spiritual earth met the physical earth. It was then that it became necessary to create vegetation. God created the physical trees, seeds, and herbs that we find on the earth. He also created the grass. The first physical creation, according to the account in Genesis, was the earth. At this point, earth in its physical creation was surrounded by nothing more than a spiritual template. It is now that we arrive at the fourth day.

THE FOURTH DAY

And God said, Let there be lights in the firmament of the heaven to divide the day from the night; and let them be for signs, and for seasons, and for days, and years: And let them be for lights in the firmament of the heaven to give light upon the earth: and it was so. And God made two great lights; the greater light to rule the day, and the lesser light to rule the night: he made the stars also. And God set them in the firmament of the heaven to give light upon the earth, and to rule over the day and over the night, and to divide the light from the darkness: and God saw that it was good. And the evening and the morning were the fourth day.

(Genesis 1:14–19)

While spiritual light is translated from the Hebrew word 'owr, we find that this passage has a different word being translated as *light*. This is the Hebrew word ma'owr. This word means "luminaries." Thus we see that the spiritual template gets populated on the fourth day. Whereas the only physical body in existence at the end of the third day was the earth, it is on the fourth day that the rest of the physical universe is brought into existence around the earth. In creating a spiritual template first, and then putting a physical creation on top of it, God does something else interesting. He successfully ties the lower parts of the spirit realm, most notably the spiritual template of our planet, to our space-time. Thus, spirits like demons that are bound upon the earth are subject to time, just like humans. They know that there is a time for their appointed judgment, and this comes out very clearly in the Bible.

"And when he was come to the other side into the country of the Gergesenes, there met him two possessed with devils, coming out of the tombs, exceeding fierce, so that no man might pass by that way. And, behold, they cried out, saying, What have we to do with thee, Jesus, thou Son of God? art thou come hither to torment us **before the time**?" (Matthew 8:28–29).

"Therefore be glad (exult), O heavens and you that dwell in them! But woe to you, O earth and sea, for the devil has come down to you in fierce anger (fury), because he knows that **he has [only] a short time [left]**!" (Revelation 12:12 AMPC).

Not all areas of the heavens are subject to time. However, the lower parts of the heavens are. This revelation helps us to understand many things. As it is written, even the devil knows that his time is short (Revelation 12:12). Conversely, God operates far beyond the limitations of time and space.

As to the question of angels, it is fairly clear that they pre-existed the physical creation. As to when they were created, I will not claim to know an answer I do not know. However, we do know that they were present when God was laying the foundation of the earth. What is the foundation of the earth? I propose that it is the spiritual template that I have been talking about all this time. The foundation of the earth is the spiritual earth upon which the physical earth has been placed. It was during its establishment and fastening that the angels were rejoicing. Consider the following passage.

"Where were you when I laid the foundation of the earth? Declare to Me, if you have and know understanding. Who determined the measures of the earth, if you know? Or who stretched the measuring line upon it? Upon what were the foundations of it fastened, or who laid its cornerstone, **When the morning stars sang together and all the sons of God [being** the heavenly hosts or angels] shouted for joy?" (Job 38:4–7 AMPC, brackets mine).

In conclusion, I believe that great revelation will open up to us as we incorporate higher dimensions into our understanding of the Bible. Regarding the physical creation, when we understand that it resides upon a spiritual template, it allows for a seamless interpretation of the creation account. It also helps us to understand some of the radical things that occur in the earth. For instance, it explains how "ghosts," or what I would call demons, can be seen in a physical house, yet have no physical nature themselves. It explains how witches can have meetings in the "astral realm" that occur in specific geographies on the physical earth (such as in a house, on a hill, or in a forest). It explains how unseen entities can be present "just one layer" behind the physical realm and then inflict sleep paralysis on an individual as they physically hold them down from the spirit realm. It even points to the significance of hypothetical things such as "Ley Lines." God is pulling back the veil in these last days and pouring out a new level of understanding and comprehension. As faithful children, we should embrace the things that God is pouring out.

It is at this time that we are prepared to move from the creation of the spiritual universe and into the structuring of the heavens themselves. While I believe it is clear that earth sits atop a spiritual template, and that creation is "layered," what are we to do with the heavens? How have the heavens been laid out and structured? Furthermore, how does dimensionality play into this conversation?

CHAPTER 3

The Heavens

In the Book of Genesis, we learned that God created the heavens and the earth. We will now transition from what God did with the earth, and into how he laid out and structured the heavens. The word translated *heavens* is plural in Genesis 1:1. It is translated from the Hebrew word *she-mayim*. This is not an accident.

"In the beginning God (prepared, formed, fashioned, and) created the **heavens** and the earth" (Genesis 1:1 AMPC).

From the very beginning, the Bible clearly establishes that multiple heavens were designed as part of the original creation. Some believe that there is nothing beyond earth and the stars of outer space. Others add to this a literal heaven and hell, but believe this to be the end of the discussion. This is a terrible oversimplification of the issue at hand. It is absolutely essential to understand the fact that there are multiple heavens and countless heavenly places. Make no mistake that there is a part of heaven that contains the literal throne of God, but this is not all there is to it.

The heavens are broken up into three main realms (2 Corinthians 12:2–4). The Bible makes this revelation pretty straightforward. The realms are defined as follows:

➢ The First Heaven

➢ The Second Heaven

➢ The Third Heaven

Before breaking each of these realms down we are going to introduce a figure to help guide our discussion.

JACOB'S LADDER AND A WORKING MODEL

The upcoming figure will help with the process of visualization. It is a model that is based in part on something called *Jacob's ladder,* which is discussed in the Book of Genesis. Here is the background. Jacob went to sleep in a particular location and had a dream. In this dream he saw the angels of God descending and ascending from heaven. The angels were descending and ascending upon a "ladder."

"And he dreamed, and behold a **ladder** set up on the earth, and the top of it reached to heaven: and behold the angels of God ascending and descending on it" (Genesis 28:12).

Most individuals will read this passage and not give it much thought. Maybe you are one of them—I know I was! Since we cannot build a literal ladder to heaven, many will simply shrug this passage off and continue reading. However, if we take a moment to ponder, we must admit that if nothing else, it is mystifying. What was Jacob actually looking at?

What I believe he saw was the layout of ascending dimensions. Even if this isn't what he actually saw in his dream, the concept still helps us to build a working model for communicating the idea of higher dimensions. Do not expect to completely understand the figure right now. Use it as a reference point as you familiarize yourself with the concepts we will be discussing.

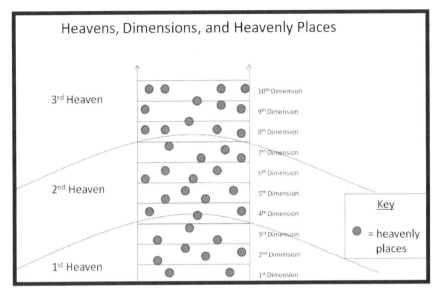

Figure 1

THE DISCLAIMER

I need to add a disclaimer that this picture is not entirely verifiable. I have no basis by which to accurately determine where the second heaven ends and where the third heaven begins. This figure employs an assumption on this issue (that it is between the seventh and eighth dimensions) for the sheer purpose of expressing the concepts that will be discussed. While we can dogmatically state that the first heaven ends at the third dimension (length, width, and height), there are no official sources that allow us to dogmatically state the breakdown of dimensions beyond the third dimension.

There is also no way to know exactly how many dimensions there are. I show ten for the sake of simplicity. Biblically, ten can represent ordinal perfection or the perfection of divine order.[1] Based on this fact, it could make sense that creation would find its pinnacle at the tenth dimension. When we consider different approaches to quantum physics, the Superstring Theory, M-Theory, and Bosonic String Theory respectively posit that there are 10, 11, and 24 dimensions.[2] In short, this is anyone's guess. I personally suspect, along with my friend and mentor Dr. Preston Bailey, that there may be thirteen dimensions. This is why I have included arrows to account for all of the potential dimensions beyond the tenth dimension. Don't worry if your head is spinning! This will all make much more sense as we proceed.

THE THIRD HEAVEN

The easiest way to explain this concept is to begin with the third heaven and work our way down. The third heaven is the highest heaven. Thus, it is expected that this is where we would find God, since he is described as the Most High God, possessor and maker of heaven and earth (Genesis 14:22). While the Bible is clear that Jesus has ascended above all heavens (Ephesians 4:10), he still enjoys an existence in the third heaven.[3] In the New Testament, the Apostle Paul was taken to this place, enabling him to give us a brief yet relatively vague description. He is speaking in the third person.

"I know a man in Christ who fourteen years ago—whether in the body or out of the body I do not know, God knows—was caught up to the **third heaven**. And I know that this man—whether in the body or away from the body I do not know, God knows—Was caught up into paradise, and he heard utterances beyond the power of man to put into words, which man is not permitted to utter" (2 Corinthians 12:2–4 AMPC).

The third heaven is the location of paradise. It is a location where Paul heard languages so beautiful that it was impossible to describe them with words. This is the area most people think about when they hear the word *heaven*. The third heaven is a place of beauty and perfection. It is here that we will find ourselves upon death if we are saved by faith in Jesus Christ. The Bible teaches that to be absent from the body is to be present with the Lord (2 Corinthians 5:8). When we die we will fully exist where he is.

Although this is the only place in the Bible where this place is named "the third heaven," it is not the only place where the Bible speaks about it. Many passages in the Bible depict scenes that are occurring in this place. The third heaven is vast, and there is much to discuss regarding it. For instance, the living creatures that praise God day and night conduct their service in the realm of the third heaven. How incredible would it be to have been John, the author of the Book of Revelation, in this moment?

After this I looked, and, behold, a door was opened in heaven: and the first voice which I heard was as it were of a trumpet talking with me; which said, Come up hither, and I will shew thee things which must be hereafter. And immediately I was in the spirit: and, behold, a throne was set in heaven, and one sat on the throne. And he that sat was to look upon like a jasper and a sardine stone: and there was a rainbow round about the throne, in sight like unto an emerald. And round about the throne were four and twenty seats: and upon the seats I saw four and twenty elders sitting, clothed in white raiment; and they had on their heads crowns of gold. And out of the throne proceeded lightnings and thunderings and voices: and there were seven lamps of fire burning before the throne, which are the seven Spirits of God. And before the throne there was a sea of glass like unto crystal: and in the midst of the throne, and round about the throne, were four beasts full of eyes before and behind. And the first beast was like a lion, and the second beast like a calf, and the third beast had a face as a man, and the fourth beast was like a flying eagle. And the four beasts had each of them six wings about him; and they were full of eyes within: and they rest not day and night, saying, Holy, holy, holy, Lord God Almighty, which was, and is, and is to come.

(Revelation 4:1-8)

This isn't the only picture we see of the third heaven. There is another account in the Book of Isaiah. On this occasion, an angel referred to as a seraphim took a coal from the altar in heaven and used it to touch the prophet's lips. This type of angelic being possessed six wings. Once the angel had finished purging the prophet's sins with the burning coal, the prophet was able to respond to God's call (see Isaiah 6).

As a lead-in to some of the concepts we will be discussing in future chapters, I want to bring attention to the following passage. While it doesn't present a picture of a specific event occurring in the third heaven, it speaks volumes of information about it. It reveals the location of the blessings that God has stored up for his children.

"Blessed be the God and Father of our Lord Jesus Christ, who hath blessed us with all spiritual blessings in **heavenly places** in Christ" (Ephesians 1:3).

Notice that we have spiritual blessings in heavenly places. The word *places* is plural for a reason. There are places within the third heaven that contain our spiritual blessings. What does this mean for us? This means that our blessings are stored up in another dimension waiting to be manifested *into* this world. In other words, they are intended to be extracted.

How are we to extract these blessings? We do this by faith. Faith connects us to the blessings of heaven.

Touching on Faith

"Now faith is the substance of things hoped for, the evidence of things not seen" (Hebrews 11:1).

In this passage we learn how the Bible defines faith. What does it mean to be the substance of things hoped for and the evidence of things not seen? First we'll take a look at the original Greek, and then we'll draw some conclusions that are, frankly, profound.

➢ *Faith* is translated from the Greek word *pistis* and means "conviction of the truth of anything." When it comes to its biblical usage, it is in reference to conviction of God's truth. We could also say that it means "to be fully persuaded."

➢ *Substance* is translated from the Greek word *hypostasis*, which means "a setting or placing under" or "that which has a foundation and is firm" (that which has an actual existence).

➢ *Evidence* is translated from the Greek word *elegchos*, which means "a proof, that by which a thing is proven or tested." The Amplified Bible renders it this way.

"Now faith is the assurance (the confirmation, the title deed) of the things [we] hope for, being the proof of things [we] do not see *and* the conviction of their reality [faith perceiving as real fact what is not revealed to the senses]" (Hebrews 11:1 AMPC).

Notice that to the word *assurance* the Amplified Bible adds the words *title deed*. A title deed indicates ownership and access by lawful rights. Faith is our title deed to the things we hope for (meaning heavenly things). It is our access by lawful right to heavenly things, and thereby becomes our "proof" or "conviction of reality." For instance, if you go to a restaurant and there is a line, they will give you a device that buzzes when it's your turn to eat. This buzzer is the equivalent of a furnished table, but it does not look like a table—it is the promise of a table. The buzzer represents faith. While you don't see the table (your heavenly thing) you have a buzzer (faith) which is proof (or conviction of the reality) that you will soon be sitting down to eat. It's really a very simple idea.

The fact of the matter is that faith is not something dormant; we show our faith by our works (James 2:22). Works include speaking God's word and responding to God with acts of obedience. In one sense, *the words we speak in faith will actually pull from the spirit realm realities that will then manifest in the natural realm.* Remember that substance pertains to that which is underlying and actually exists. You don't see it, but it is there. You don't see it because it is in another dimension.

This substance or underlying foundation that cannot be seen is *evidence* that the things we call forth will manifest from the unseen realm. Remember that *evidence* means "proof." When we act in faith, God moves. In this way, faith becomes a sort of *currency*. We exchange our faith for the manifestation of God's works. The amount of faith that we have equals the amount of power that we will walk in. Faith is a powerful force.

I remember one occasion when I found myself praying for a fellow server at a restaurant where I was working. He had formerly undergone several back surgeries, but nothing could solve the problem of his perpetual pain due to problems in his lower back. One day the pain was unbearable. I found him sitting down in the middle of his shift, unable to continue waiting on his tables. I asked him if he believed that Jesus could heal him. When he said yes, I didn't waste any time. I put my hand on his shoulder and said a quick sixty-second prayer while we released our faith for his healing. Afterwards, I told him to stand up, and he did! Enough healing manifested in that moment for him to finish his shift.

After our shift was over, God told me to prophesy to him. I was to tell him that by the time he woke up the next day, it would be as if his back had never been injured at all. This was nerve-racking for me, but I decided to choose faith instead of fear. I stepped out in obedience and delivered the prophetic word. The result: he woke up the next day with a fully restored back. Praise God! To my knowledge, his back never gave him a problem again. By exchanging faith for the manifestation of God's works, faith became the substance of things hoped for and the evidence of things not seen.

MORE ON THE THIRD HEAVEN

In the third heaven we are seated with Christ in heavenly places. To be *seated* is to "rest from our labors." Jesus has made us to rest in him (Hebrews 4:10). Although we may not be experiencing rest on this earth, in the third heaven, where a Christian's spirit is presently located, it truly is "seated with Christ." Notice that the word *places* is again made plural. Just like there are multiple places in the earth, there are multiple places in the third heaven.

"And hath raised us up together, and made us sit together in heavenly places in Christ Jesus" (Ephesians 2:6).

It is a revelatory thought to understand that our spirit has a life we are not conscious of. While we will explore this idea later on, suffice it to say that our spirit interacts with heaven on a daily basis when we are saved by grace through faith in Jesus Christ (Ephesians 2:8–9). If this were not so, the Bible would not say that he *has* raised us up. The verb tense clearly indicates a past action. The Bible is not speaking to a future event for the believer. We are participating in heaven right now! The work of God is simply spectacular.

THE SECOND HEAVEN

We are now going to define the second heaven. The second heaven comprises all of the dimensions that exist beneath those of the third heaven, but above the first heaven. Although this division is visualized as occurring between the 7th and 8th dimensions in our figure, this assumption is pure guesswork. Where this division actually occurs is irrelevant to our study. What we must understand is that it is in this sphere of existence that we find dark powers. Lucifer (otherwise known as Satan) and the rest of his evil hierarchy work out of these dimensions in one way or another. The second heaven contains multiple dimensions, and similar to the third heaven, also has places.

"For we are not wrestling with flesh and blood [contending only with physical opponents], but against the despotisms, against the powers, against [the master spirits who are] the world rulers of this present darkness, against the spirit forces of wickedness in the heavenly (supernatural) sphere" (Ephesians 6:12 AMPC).

The second heaven is just as full of activity as the third heaven. It is incredible to try and wrap our minds around how much is occurring "just over our heads," so to speak. There are agendas being executed constantly in these other dimensions, and we just so happen to be at the center of it all. How important are these higher dimensions to our lives? Their importance *cannot* be overstated. One example of an agenda involving these places is

God's agenda to reveal his wisdom <u>to</u> the heavenly hosts <u>with</u> the Church (those saved by grace through faith in Jesus Christ). This thought is one for deep meditation.

"To the intent that now unto the principalities and powers in **heavenly places** might be known by the church the manifold wisdom of God" (Ephesians 3:10).

It is important to realize that God's angels also execute agendas in the second heaven. In other words: *it is a warzone.* This comes out ever so clearly in the Book of Daniel. The story goes that Daniel went on a twenty-one day fast in order to seek the Lord on a matter. His answer came in the form of an angelic messenger. When the messenger arrived, it was explained to Daniel that he was withheld twenty-one days by the prince of Persia. It is virtually a universal understanding that the prince of Persia was a powerful fallen angel, not a human prince. This battle did not come to resolution until another archangel, named Michael, came to assist. This illustrates the point that both Godly and satanic activity occurs in the second heaven.

"Therefore I was left alone, and saw this great vision, and there remained no strength in me: for my comeliness was turned in me into corruption, and I retained no strength... And, behold, an hand touched me, which set me upon my knees and upon the palms of my hands... Then said he unto me, Fear not, Daniel: for from the first day that thou didst set thine heart to understand, and to chasten thyself before thy God, thy words were heard, and I am come for thy words. But the prince of the kingdom of Persia withstood me one and twenty days: but, lo, Michael, one of the chief princes, came to help me; and I remained there with the kings of Persia" (Daniel 10:8, 10, 12–13).

The First Heaven

With the third heaven and second heaven defined, it leaves us with the first heaven. What is the first heaven? With basic logic you have probably already guessed that it is the world in which we live. This is absolutely correct. *The first heaven encompasses all life that exists within earth's atmosphere.* In the following passages, the fowls are spoken of as being of the heaven. Which heaven do birds fly in? Birds are residents of the earth like the rest of creation, and fly in the space between earth's atmosphere and earth's surface. They fly within the first heaven. The first heaven is found in the carnal realm where people and animals dwell.

"And God said, Let the waters bring forth abundantly the moving creature that hath life, and fowl that may fly above the earth in the open firmament of heaven" (Genesis 1:20)

"I will consume man and beast; I will consume the fowls of the heaven, and the fishes of the sea, and the stumbling blocks with the wicked: and I will cut off man from off the land, saith the LORD" (Zephaniah 1:3).

Pulling it All Together

This is all reinforced by a single verse in the Old Testament. It is a hidden gem that is all too often overlooked. The Bible says of God that to him belongs the "heavens," "the heaven of heavens," and also "the earth." The "heaven of heavens" can be understood as another reference to the third heaven; "heaven" can be understood as a reference to the second heaven; and "the earth" would then be a reference to the first heaven.

"Behold, the **heaven** and the **heaven of heavens** is the Lord's thy God, **the earth** also, with all that therein is" (Deuteronomy 10:14).

In the following figure, the layout of ascending heavens is clarified. When moving from the first heaven to the second heaven, we are not traveling a distance. Instead, we are entering into a realm that *contains* the first heaven. The same goes when moving from the second heaven to the third heaven. They are not separated by distance because the third heaven contains the second heaven and the first heaven.

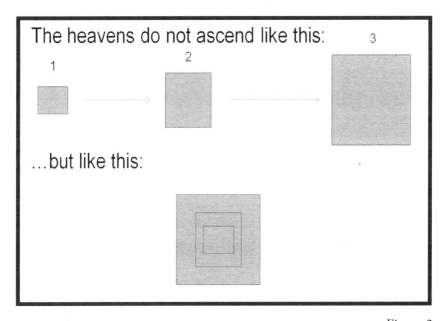

Figure 2

CHAPTER 4

Higher Dimensions versus Parallel Dimensions

To briefly summarize our discussion up to this point; the first heaven is all that is contained by earth's atmosphere, the second heaven contains higher dimensions where dark powers are found and spiritual battles rage, and the third heaven is the realm of paradise. Thus, we have effectively described the three heavens. Nonetheless, we have yet to answer the question: how do dimensions work?

HIGHER DIMENSIONS

A brief glance at the figure from the last chapter will reveal the three heavens, heavenly places, and also dimensions. In order to understand how dimensions work, think about it like this. In our world, I can put a dot on a piece of paper. The dot is a zero-dimensional unit. In theory, it has no dimensions. However, I can put a large number of dots in a row and create a line. This line will have one measure, which is length. Thus, it can be said that a line is a one-dimensional unit. Now consider the paper that it is drawn on. The paper can *contain* the one-dimensional line because it has two dimensions: length and width. The one-dimensional line is contained by the two-dimensional paper. Due to the fact that they exist on different dimensional planes they can interact with each other, overlap, yet not collide.

Now consider the two-dimensional paper with the one-dimensional line. If I hang this up in a three-dimensional room, both the paper and the line are contained by the higher dimension, which has length, width, and height (the room). Now the line, the paper, and the room are all interacting with each other, overlapping, and yet not colliding. With each step we are introducing a higher dimension. This pattern continues into the fourth dimension, the fifth dimension, and so forth. It is much more difficult to create a word picture for how this works in higher dimensions. However, suffice it to say that the fourth dimension contains the third, the fifth contains the fourth, and so on. This is why activity occurring in higher dimensions can easily be hidden from us.

Only when two objects exist on the same dimensional plane do events like collisions become possible. For instance, if I try to draw two squares on the same piece of paper, and I attempt to draw them in the same place, there will be collision. The lines that are used to create one square will collide with the lines used to create the other square. If I move up to the third dimension I will observe similar things. Let's say I want to put boxes in the exact same place on a desk. As I slide the two boxes together they will make contact. While I will be able to stack the boxes, I will be unable to make them occupy the same exact place at the same time. The principle is that objects with the same number of dimensions can collide. This principle remains the same when moving into the fourth dimension and beyond as well.

PARALLEL DIMENSIONS

Parallel dimensions are easier to understand once the concept of higher dimensions has been defined. Up until this point we have been solely discussing the implications of higher dimensions. Only now is it relevant to bring into our discussion the issue of parallel dimensions. They are different than higher dimensions, and I want to make sure that there is a distinction in terms. Higher dimensions involve adding dimensions (adding width to length, adding height to width, etc.). *Parallel dimensions have the same number of dimensions while existing in alternate space within higher dimensions.* Let me explain.

Let's say I take a two-dimensional piece of paper and draw a line on it. This means that I have both a one-dimensional unit (the line) and a two-dimensional unit (the paper). In moving from the line to the paper, I am ascending to a higher dimension. This is what we have just discussed. However, if I draw a second line on that paper next to the first line, I now have two one-dimensional units and one two-dimensional unit. I have just created a parallel dimension. The second line, because it exists on a lower dimensional plane than the paper that contains it, becomes parallel to the original line. The two one-dimensional lines are parallel dimensions. *They have the same number of dimensions while existing in alternate space within a higher dimension.*

Moving up, let's say I have two squares in a room. Those two squares are each two dimensions (length and width). If I stack them next to each other I am again viewing parallel dimensions. The dimensions of length and width define the two-dimensional squares. They can both exist in a three-dimensional environment without ever having any type of interaction. The only way interaction becomes possible is if three-dimensional space can be crossed, or if the squares are forced to overlap (or collide) within the three-dimensional space. This same concept continues into the fourth dimension, the fifth dimension, and so forth. This means that within four-dimensional space, the concept of multiple earths and alternate three-dimensional universes is theoretically possible. Moving up to the fifth dimension gets much more mind-bending.

Outer Space

Thus, we have established a basic understanding of the three realms of heaven and how heavenly places are best understood as actual locations found in higher dimensions. We have also defined the distinction between higher dimensions and parallel dimensions. However, at this point you may be asking yourself, "If the first heaven is all that is contained by earth's atmosphere, and the second heaven begins at the fourth dimension, what does that make outer space?" This is a good question, and one that I have admittedly been back and forth on. Frankly, it doesn't seem to me that one *must* be in four-dimensional space to have entered the second heaven. Although I mentioned it in passing, my conclusion, as of writing this book, is that outer space falls into the category of the second heaven, although the planets and comets still exist according the same three-dimensional properties of earth. I believe this is suggested by the following Scriptures.

"And they shall spread them before **the sun, and the moon, and all the host of heaven**, whom they have loved, and whom they have served, and after whom they have walked, and whom they have sought, and whom they have worshipped: they shall not be gathered, nor be buried; they shall be for dung upon the face of the earth" (Jeremiah 8:2).

"For the **stars of heaven and the constellations thereof** shall not give their light: the sun shall be darkened in his going forth, and the moon shall not cause her light to shine" (Isaiah 13:10).

The best way to understand what is going on is to go back to the spiritual template described in Chapter 2. Earth is layered, with the physical realm resting on top of a spiritual template. The same principle is established in respect to the planets and stars. There is a physical overlay that rests upon a spiritual template that was stretched out during creation. Therefore, outer space is truly multidimensional in nature, just like earth.

In speaking with individuals who have defected from the kingdom of darkness, I have learned some very interesting things. One of these pieces of information specifically relates to the mechanics of outer space. It has been reported to me that it is possible to astrally project and be out-of-body in the physical earth or in outer space. When these individuals were out-of-body with others in outer space, they report appearing physical to each other. However, if one were to view them from the third dimension, they would not be seen. This occurs because of the multidimensional layering that exists in outer space.

Now that we have effectively defined the three heavens, heavenly places, and dimensions, we will begin to explore our interaction with them. This will take us into a deep assessment of the conscious mind, the subconscious mind, and the unconscious mind. However, before we dive into that study, we will spend some more time getting a firm grasp of dimensionality. In order to do this, we will establish a foundational approach to understanding the first four spatial dimensions.

CHAPTER 5

The First Four Spatial Dimensions

"That you may have the power *and* be strong to apprehend *and* grasp with all the saints [God's devoted people, the experience of that love] what is the **breadth** and **length** and **height** and **depth** [of it]" (Ephesians 3:18 AMPC).

A dimension is to be understood as a property of space or an extension in a given direction.[4] In this powerful verse, the Apostle Paul describes the love of God as possessing four dimensions. Breadth, length, depth, and height each represent one extension in a given direction for a total of four dimensions. In order to understand how we actually move beyond the third dimension, it helps to introduce some visual illustrations. This chapter, beginning at the theoretical "0" dimension, will walk you through the first, second, and third dimensions. It will then provide you with a visual expression of a four-dimensional object known as a tesseract or hypercube. The goal is to prepare your mind to stretch beyond three-dimensional confines in order to get a better grasp of the concepts that will be described as this book progresses. In the end, this chapter will not only explain how to understand higher spatial dimensions, but will even train you to draw a four-dimensional object.

NOTE TO READER: If math and science are not your strong points, feel free to skip this chapter! While it serves to set a good foundation, it is not necessary in order to understand the rest of the book and the concepts that will be presented.

The "0" Dimension

In the first figure below, you will find a visual expression of the "0" dimension. This is represented by a simple dot or point. In actuality, were one to look at the "0" dimension, the point would not even be visible because in order to appear visible, it would require both length and height. Therefore, understand that the point is only a theoretical representation of the "0" dimension. You will also notice a small box in the figure that serves as a key. It is for the purpose of showing the directions of measurement present in the illustration. With no dimensions, there is no axis present in the box. The "0" dimension has no measurement in any direction—thus being represented by a simple point in space.

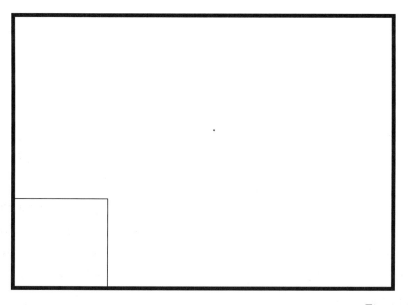

Figure 3

THE FIRST DIMENSION

As we work our way up, we enter the first dimension. This is the dimension of length. In math, this dimensions is often measured on what is called the x-axis. For this reason, we will also include the x-axis in our key. We represent the first dimension with a single line. In theory, the first dimension would not be visible, just like the "0" dimension, because to create a line on paper actually requires both length and height, even though the height is less than one millimeter. However, for the purposes of our discussion, a line will suffice as a good representation of the first dimension.

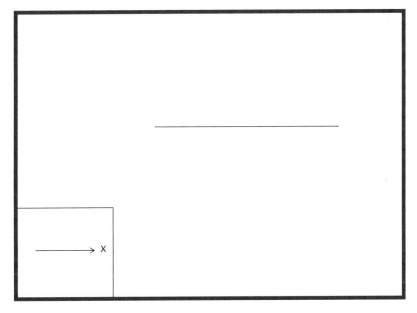

Figure 4

The first dimension of length is able to theoretically house an infinite number of individual points. This inherent quality of a line (or the measure of length) begins a pattern that we observe as we move up from one dimension to the next. In theory, higher dimensions can always house an infinite number of lower dimensional objects, spaces, or locations. In this case, an infinite number of points (representing solitary locations in space) can be contained by a measure of length.

Below I have shown a representation of the first dimension. It has been deconstructed to show how it is comprised of "0" dimensional elements. These are represented as a series of dots. Keep in mind that the representation of dots is misleading because these dots, in order to be seen, have a small length and height. The purpose of the picture is to communicate the principle.

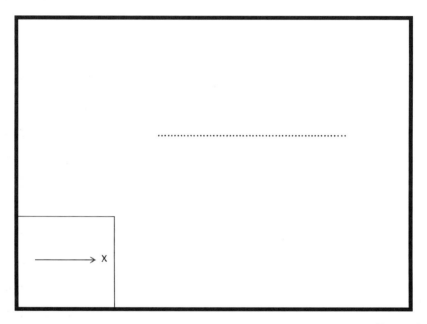

Figure 5

THE SECOND DIMENSION

In order to move up from the first dimension, we have to add a dimension. Simply put, we will be adding height to length. This is represented by the y-axis in math. For this reason, we will show the x-axis and y-axis in the key. If you're like most Americans, you probably remember having to learn how to utilize graphs and charts based on the combination of these two dimensions. I know I do! The second dimension is familiar territory for virtually all of us.

Interestingly enough, while we live in a three-dimensional world, we only perceive two dimensions. In order to process three-dimensional realities, we actually have to rely upon points of reference, shadows, reflections, and experience. If you are slightly taken aback by this concept, simply answer this question: When you are talking with your friend and they are facing you, can you see their backside and front side simultaneously? Of course not. This is impossible without the use of mirrors (or by filming their backside with a camera and displaying the live feed on your phone!)

What about your house? Can you stand in your front yard and see the opposite side of your home? If you can, your house is undoubtedly in really bad condition. It would literally require the back of the home to be ripped out of its foundation and removed to a location where it is resting next to the front entrance.

In any case, to truly see in three dimensions requires that we have the ability to observe all sides of a three-dimensional object at once. This would require us to actually be looking at three-dimensional objects from the fourth dimension. From a fourth-dimensional perspective, one would be able to see all sides of a three-dimensional object at once, just like from a three-dimensional perspective we can view all sides of a two-dimensional object at once. Now let's look at our two-dimensional object. You should immediately recognize it as a square.

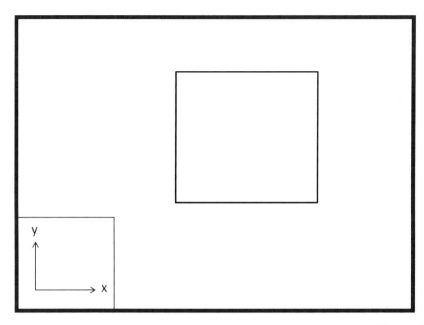

Figure 6

This square requires the dimensions of length and height to be present before it can exist. Without height, two-dimensional objects cannot exist—they're just lines of length. Keep in mind that the same principle we observed in moving from zero dimensions to one dimension remains true here. While the square is formed by four lines, as a two-dimensional plane it can theoretically contain an infinite number of one-dimensional units. Nonetheless, it only requires four lines to actually assemble the shape of a square. When we disassemble the two-dimensional square into its one-dimensional components, we wind up with four lines of equal length.

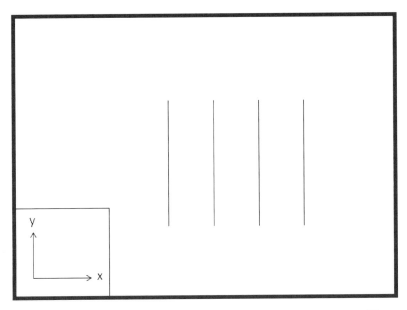

Figure 7

In order for these lines to form a square they must follow a simple rule. Each line must be parallel to one line and perpendicular to the other two lines. To be parallel means to be extending in the same direction.[5] To be perpendicular means to meet a line or surface at a right angle (meaning an angle measuring 90 degrees).[6] This leads us to a simple equation that shows us just how many lines are required to create a square. There is one reference line, two lines perpendicular, and one line parallel. This gives us the equation of $1+2+1=4$.[7] Thus, we have four sides to a square.

THE THIRD DIMENSION

When we add the dimension of width to the second dimension, we arrive at the third dimension. The dimension of width is often represented by the z-axis in mathematics. In the key, you will find an x-axis representing length, a y-axis representing height, and the z-axis representing width. We will represent the third dimension with a cube. A cube is formed by assembling six squares together. Each square will be parallel to one square and perpendicular to the other four.

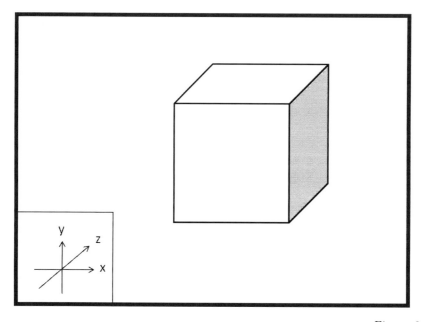

Figure 8

In three dimensions, all axes reside at 90 degrees from all other axes. In two dimensions, the axes were also positioned at 90 degrees from each other. In the picture above, while the z-axis *appears* to be at 45 degrees from the x-axis and y-axis, we understand that it represents a direction on a third dimension. It is actually coming towards you and moving away from you. In order to represent this property on a two-dimensional surface (the paper), it requires that the z-axis be _set_ at an angle it does not represent (45 degrees), and _defined_ by the angle that it does represent (90 degrees). Due to the way our eyes perceive our three-dimensional environment on a daily basis, this logic will immediately make sense to the vast majority of people.

In order to solve the question of how many sides a cube has, we can use the same logic that we applied to the square. We begin with a reference square. This square has four edges that must be shared by squares assembled perpendicular to the reference square. In order to complete the shape, there needs to be one square that rests parallel to the reference square and perpendicular to the same four. Thus, it yields the equation 1+4+1=6.[8] When we deconstruct the cube, this is exactly what we find to be true. Keep in mind that while it takes six squares to *frame* a cube, a cube can theoretically *contain* an infinite number of squares.

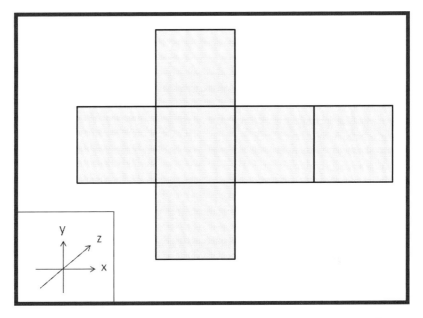

Figure 9

Thus far we have created two very simple equations. The equation of 1+2+1=4 helped us to comprehend why there are four sides to a square. The equation of 1+4+1=6 helped us to comprehend why there are six sides to a cube. You may be thinking this is obvious, but the logic will help us to define our next shape, which actually occurs in four-dimensional space. This shape is called a hypercube or a tesseract. I have created two pictures of this shape in order to display it from two separate perspectives.

The Fourth Dimension

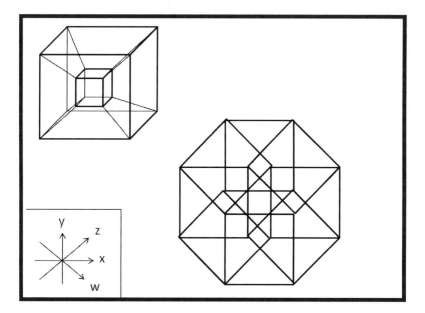

Figure 10

The casual observer would probably not assume that these pictures represent four-dimensional shapes. Why should they? The upper left picture looks like a box suspended within a box. The lower right picture looks like a neat pattern. So what qualifies these pictures as representations of a four-dimensional shape? The answer is the fact that they are defined and plotted against a four-dimensional axis.

In the key of this figure you will find that a fourth axis has been added and labeled as the w-axis. It appears to be 45 degrees from the x-axis, just like the z-axis appears to be 45 degree from the x-axis. The fact of the matter is that this is only a representation of its direction. Remember that when we added the z-axis, we had to define it as resting at 90 degrees from both of the other two axes. This makes sense to most of us since we experience perspective on a daily basis. It is easy to understand three-dimensional qualities presented as two-dimensional representations because we see in two dimensions as it is. When we are told to believe that the z-axis represents a dimension moving towards and away from us it is easy to accept. It follows that we have no problem accepting that it rests perpendicular to both the x-axis and the y-axis.

Here is where the mind must begin to stretch. The w-axis as pictured in our key actually represents a dimension that rests at 90 degrees to all of the other axes. It is 90 degrees from the x-axis, 90 degrees from the y-axis, and 90 degrees from the z-axis. How can this be possible? It is possible because we have *added another dimension*. We have exited three-dimensional representations and entered four-dimensional representations. I keep using the word *representations* because it is impossible to actually show you a four-dimensional shape. In order to do that we would need to be physically present in a four-dimensional environment (or higher). Thus, we simply have to accept the logic and the principles as they are presented.

Isn't Time the Fourth Dimension?

Before proceeding, it is necessary to address an important question that some will immediately have, particularly if they have studied quantum field theory in the past. This is the question of time, because many have figured time to be a fourth dimension. This would render what I have just introduced (in displaying a hypercube) as the fifth dimension. While this logic is acceptable by some standards, what I am doing in my approach is essential separating types of dimensions. Spatial dimensions are extensions in a given direction such as length, depth, and height. A temporal dimension is a way by which events are ordered from the past through the present and into the future.[9] Time is a temporal dimension, and for this reason I have excluded it from the conversation on spatial dimensions. Keep in mind that in authoring this book I am not declaring myself to be an expert on the science behind quantum field theory. I am simply introducing some basic mathematical and scientific concepts in order to provide a foundation for the ideas that we will be discussing in future chapters. Refraining from labelling time as the "official fourth dimension" works to simplify the discussion. A hypercube is a representation of the fourth spatial dimension.

WHAT ABOUT GRAVITY?

In addition to time, another significant element of the discussion on time-space and quantum field theory is gravity. Gravity is certainly an intriguing subject that is extremely complex. While it plays into the discussion of quantum field theory in substantial ways, it is still an area under significant research. What this author understands about gravity is that it is the weakest of the four fundamental forces that govern nature (the other three being electromagnetism, and the nuclear strong force and weak force). It has been hypothesized that it is governed by a massless sub-atomic particle known as a graviton. Gravity is a natural phenomenon by which all physical bodies attract each other.[10] However, because it is evident that gravity is tied to the sub-atomic (or quantum) world, it follows that gravity can and does have ramifications on both time and space. On this note I leave the reader to do their own research if they are so inclined.

UNDERSTANDING A FOUR-DIMENSIONAL SHAPE

When we are looking at the representation of a hypercube, we are actually looking at a grouping of distorted cubes. Allow me to explain. Consider a six-sided die, the kind you roll to play board games. You will find it visualized in the following figure.

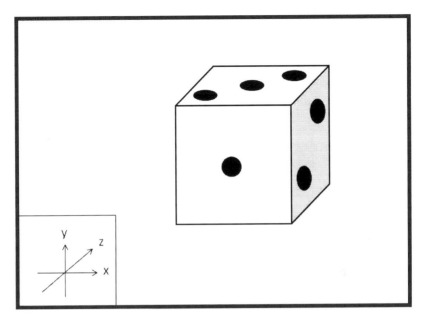

Figure 11

Assume that the die is placed a few inches from your face and that the "one" side of the die is flush with the angle of your eyes. As you look at the die, you will see that the face of the "one" side of the die is a perfect square. Furthermore, it will be impossible for you to see any other side of the die. As a matter of fact, if the rest of the die wasn't there you would be none the wiser. This works because a cube is formed by six equal squares.

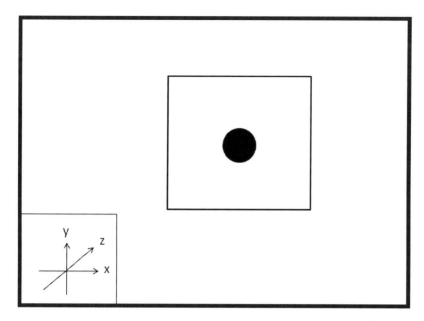

Figure 12

Imagine that the die is rotated 45 degrees. Now the "one" side of the die and the "two" side of the die are both clearly visible. The part of the die that is closest to you is the edge where the "one" side of the die and the "two" side of the die meet perpendicular to each other. While you know that each of the faces of the die are actually perfect squares, what you see no longer *appear* as perfect squares at all. If you did not have it in mind that you were looking at a three dimensional object, it would actually be possible to conclude that you are looking at two rectangles.

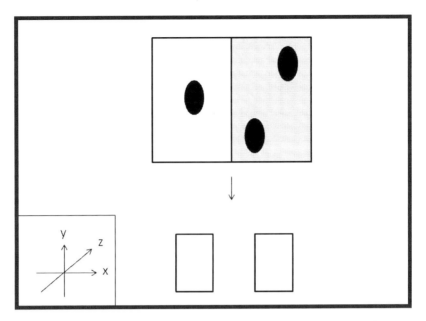

Figure 13

The fact of the matter is that the die is still a cube, and each of its faces are still perfect squares. The only thing that changed was the <u>per-spective</u>. If we define our perspective of the three-dimensional die with two-dimensional principles, the only thing we can conclude is that we are looking at two rectangles side by side. Once we realize that we are looking at a three-dimensional object, we immediately understand that it is our *perspective* of the squares that make them appear as rectangles. When we relate what we see to a three-dimensional axis, we can draw accurate conclusions. Let's consider another angle of the same three-dimensional die.

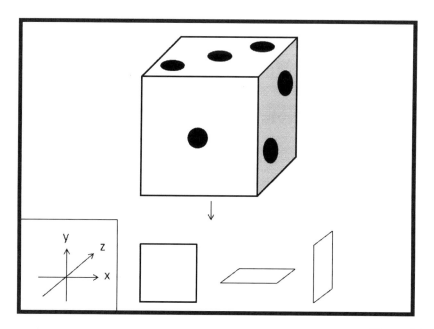

Figure 14

From this angle we are able to observe three faces of the die. As the picture shows, each face appears to be a different shape due to the distorting effect of the perspective. While we know that each face is actually a square, when we impose two-dimensional principles upon the picture we actually get one square and two parallelograms. Parallelograms are simply four-sided shapes with two sets of parallel sides. Their definition does not require their sides to meet at 90 degree angles (unlike that of squares and rectangles). The point is that our perspective skews our ability to recognize the shapes that we are actually looking at. Ultimately, we must accept that it is necessary to know how many dimensions are being represented by the object we are looking at before we presume upon what we are seeing.

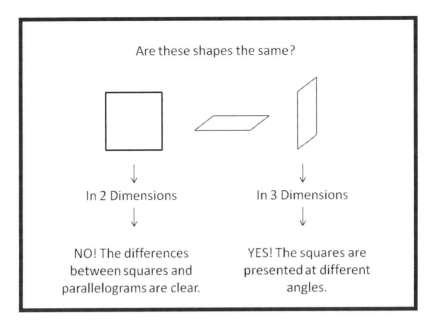

Figure 15

This figure asks a simple question: are these shapes the same? The answer is self-explanatory. They are the same shape in three dimensions, but if we restrict the consideration to two dimensions, they are not. The purpose of this exercise is to help you grasp the principles that are necessary to process four-dimensional shapes. When we look at their representation on a two-dimensional medium, we must accept that we are looking at a skewed perspective. Below is a picture that asks the same question as above. The only difference is that the shapes in question appear three-dimensional.

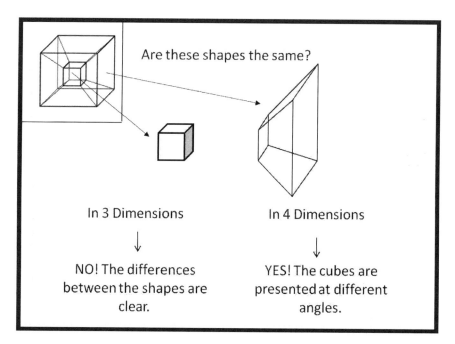

Are these shapes the same?

In 3 Dimensions   In 4 Dimensions
↓   ↓
NO! The differences between the shapes are clear.   YES! The cubes are presented at different angles.

Figure 16

In the same way that a two-dimensional perspective of a three-dimensional object skews our perspective of what we are looking at, a two-dimensional perspective of a four-dimensional object does the same thing. When I represented the hypercube earlier, one of the illustrations appeared to be a box suspended in a larger box. In the picture above, one of the sides of this hypercube has been extracted. The point is to illustrate that it is a cube, regardless of the fact that it looks like a decapitated pyramid sitting on its side. *This cube, when being viewed as part of the representation of a four-dimensional shape, is skewed in the same way that the sides of the die were skewed when viewed from different perspectives.*

A hypercube is formed by framing cubes together in the same way that a cube is formed by framing squares together. How many cubes frame a hypercube? We can posit that since there are six faces to a cube, the reference cube would by necessity reside perpendicular to six other cubes. It would follow that it would remain parallel to another cube that rested perpendicular to the same six other cubes. This is undoubtedly difficult to imagine, because it requires that we perceive something we cannot physically see or interact with. Nevertheless, we can use a simple equation to figure out how many cubes form a hypercube. This equation is 1+6+1=8.[11] Thus, while a square is 1+2+1=4 lines, a cube is 1+4+1=6 squares, and a hypercube is 1+6+1=8 cubes, the figure below pictures a deconstructed hypercube. Keep in mind that while it takes eight cubes to *frame* a hypercube, a hypercube can theoretically *contain* an infinite number of cubes.

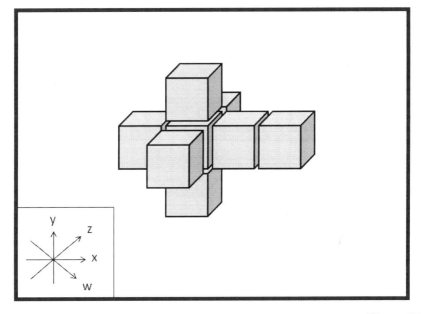

Figure 17

There are several lessons to take away from this chapter. The first is to understand that a dimension is a property of space or an extension in a given direction. The second is to understand how one can move from one dimension to the next. The third is to create a framework for understanding the rest of this book. Our physical body resides on a three-dimensional plane. Events that occur in our plane according to three-dimensional principles are what we consider "natural." Events that occur in our plane according to higher dimensional principles or as a result of higher dimensional influences are considered "supernatural." Thus, the study of higher dimensions really becomes a study of the supernatural, or what we call the spirit realm.

I want to include some brief instructions before closing out this chapter. Drawing a tesseract is actually a lot easier than one might think. After reading this chapter and working your way through the following step-by-step instructions, you'll not only be able to explain the fourth dimension, you'll also be able to draw its representation. It will allow you to spread the news to family, friends, and coworkers, regardless of whether you're at a coffee shop or in a math lab. However, don't get too excited yet! We are only at the very beginning of our journey into higher dimensions, parallel dimensions, and the spirit realm. Our next subjects of study: the conscious, subconscious, and unconscious mind.

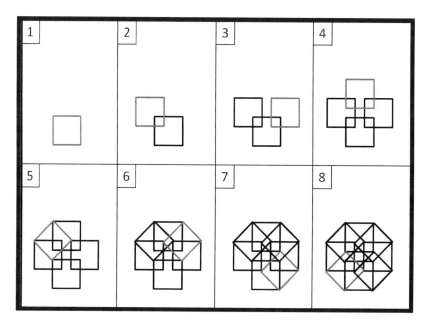

Figure 18

CHAPTER 6

The Conscious Mind

The conscious mind contains, processes, and organizes the thoughts that we have direct access to. It resides in the realm of the human soul. According to the Bible, we are made up of three major components. The soul is one of these three components, the other two being the body and the spirit.

"And the very God of peace sanctify you wholly; and I pray God your whole **spirit** and **soul** and **body** be preserved blameless unto the coming of our Lord Jesus Christ" (1 Thessalonians 5:23).

We are divided up between spirit, soul, and body. God's intent is that all three elements be preserved blameless unto the coming of Jesus Christ. As we will come to understand, there is also a fourth realm known as the heart. It operates as a gateway, or processing unit between the soul and the spirit. *The soul is most easily defined as the mind, the will, and the emotions.*

Before we proceed any further, I am going to provide you with another figure. Like the first figure, do not expect to understand it just yet. This figure will serve as a reference point for what we will be discussing in the following chapters.

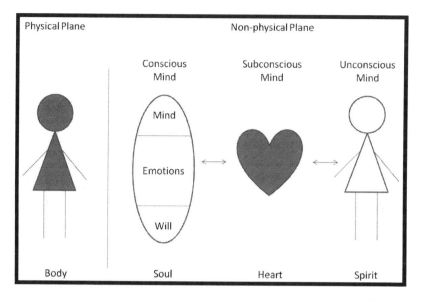

Figure 19

The body is the only element of our nature that exists on the physical plane. The easiest way to explain this is to go back to the example from the first chapter. Two squares cannot occupy the same exact place on a two-dimensional plane (a piece of paper) without colliding. Similarly, should a large object fall on my body, the object will crush me. I cannot occupy the same three-dimensional space as the large object. However, can the object fall on my emotions? Can the object crush my will? No. My emotions and my will, along with the source of my conscious thoughts, are operating on another plane—an immaterial plane. To make it simple, while we understand that our bodies operate on the physical plane, any operations that are not restricted to this plane can be considered non-physical. While we could employ the use of the term "metaphysical" in place of the term "non-physical," I prefer to not use that term due to its affiliation with belief systems that I do not endorse.

Processing Information

The conscious mind is designed to operate according to earthly realities. It exists as an element of our soul. It works hand-in-hand with our brain in order to execute its functionality. It takes in information from our three-dimensional world and processes that information according to three-dimensional paradigms. The mind develops according to experiences, memories, and standard learning procedures. While it can take in and process all sorts of contradictory information and sort through many thoughts touching on many things, little of what actually passes through our conscious mind impacts our true belief system.

For instance, when I was in college, I majored in microbiology. One of the standard aspects of any degree in the hard sciences was instruction on the theory of evolution. I had to take an entire course on this single subject and use its assumptions throughout much of my other coursework. I learned a lot of information about evolution, and I even regurgitated that information to pass my tests. However, because I believed in God and the Bible, that information did not enter my belief system. It was simply contradictory information being processed and understood by my conscious mind.

The important thing to understand about the conscious mind is that its dominant thoughts often speak to our underlying belief system. In other words, if I am always dwelling on the failures that I have experienced in my life, it is highly likely that I believe that I am a failure in my underlying belief system. This is a problem. If my thoughts are always veering towards negativity it is very difficult, and in some cases impossible, to live a fulfilled and satisfying life, even if Jesus has become my personal Lord and Savior.

Renewing the Mind

This leads to the concept of renewing our minds. The purpose of renewing our minds is to change our dominant thought patterns on purpose. When this happens, it becomes possible to change our belief system, which is better understood as our subconscious (or heart). We will be discussing this in greater detail in the next chapter. When it comes to renewing our conscious mind, the Bible says the following.

"And be not conformed to this world: but be ye transformed by the **renewing of your mind**, that ye may prove what is that good, and acceptable, and perfect, will of God" (Romans 12:2).

When our dominant thought patterns are out of line with God's desires for us, then we cannot manifest his will for our lives. Conversely, when we forcefully change the thoughts that we think with our conscious minds, it eventually changes our belief system. When this happens, we are transformed. To be *transformed* means "to be changed from one form to another form." In other words, we are changed from the form that the world has left us in and into the form that God desires for us. This allows us to prove "what is the good, and acceptable, and perfect will of God."

When we consider the process of transformation, it helps to look at a model that most of us can identify with. Butterflies are beautiful and graceful creatures. Seeing them float around is really a very pleasant thing. However, seeing them in their larval form prior to transformation is not. When we are operating out of a mind that has not been renewed we are like the disgusting larval form of the butterfly.

As we begin the process of renewing our mind, it is like entering the cocoon phase of the butterfly's life. There is a lot going on, but it is all internal. All one can observe is the cocoon's exterior, which isn't much of an improvement from the larvae. However, when the butterfly emerges after the completion of its transformation, it can be breathtaking. This is the will of God for every butterfly, and only once they emerge from their cocoon have they "proven" it. The process of transforming our conscious minds with the word of God will allow us to emerge from the process with a great degree of internal beauty and grace. It is a work that others will not be able to help but admire.

There is another interesting verse in the Bible that speaks to renewing our minds. However, it refers to something called the *spirit* of our mind. What does this imply?

"Strip yourselves of your former nature [put off and discard your old unrenewed self] which characterized your previous manner of life and becomes corrupt through lusts and desires that spring from delusion; And be constantly renewed in the **spirit of your mind** [having a fresh mental and spiritual attitude], And put on the new nature (the regenerate self) created in God's image, [Godlike] in true righteousness and holiness" (Ephesians 4:22–24 AMPC).

The Amplified Bible does a great job of bringing out the meaning of the phrase used here. The spirit of our mind is the mental and spiritual attitude that we reflect. This attitude needs to not only be renewed as a one-time event, *but as an ongoing lifestyle,* as the language indicates. It is our responsibility, if we want to keep our conscious mind in line with God's will for our lives, to renew it as a lifestyle. We must forcefully purpose to maintain a standard in our thinking that pleases God.

Renewing our mind isn't just for the purpose of having positive thoughts on practical things. It is also for the purpose of being able to accept and comprehend spiritual things. It takes work to conform our conscious mind to spiritual things. This is illustrated in the responses that Jesus received to many of the things he said. For example, when he was explaining the new birth to Nicodemus, Nicodemus thought Jesus was telling him to reenter his mother's womb. He didn't understand that Jesus was implying that our *spirit* needed to experience a new birth in order to inherit salvation and become the son (or daughter) of God.

"There was a man of the Pharisees, named Nicodemus, a ruler of the Jews: The same came to Jesus by night, and said unto him, Rabbi, we know that thou art a teacher come from God: for no man can do these miracles that thou doest, except God be with him. Jesus answered and said unto him, Verily, verily, I say unto thee, except a man be born again, he cannot see the kingdom of God. Nicodemus saith unto him, how can a man be born when he is old? Can he enter the second time into his mother's womb, and be born?" (John 3:1–4).

Preparing to Comprehend the Spirit Realm

As we journey into the concept of higher dimensions, it will be necessary to renew our minds to spiritual things. Apart from doing this it will be impossible to understand our interaction with the spirit realm. However, once we can grasp these spiritual things and begin to perceive them not only consciously, but also subconsciously, it will become possible for us to manifest things that are absolutely spectacular. For instance, at what level does the interpretation of the following saying become literal? When does faith become effective enough to see literal mountains cast into the sea?

"For verily I say unto you, That whosoever shall say unto this mountain, Be thou removed, and be thou cast into the sea; and shall not doubt in his **heart**, but shall believe that those things which he saith shall come to pass; he shall have whatsoever he saith" (Mark 11:23).

Once we understand that the activity in the spirit realm is more real than what we experience in this world, wonders like this <u>will</u> enter the realm of possibility. Jesus walked through walls (John 20:19), cloaked himself in invisibility (John 8:59), walked on water (Matthew 14:25), and literally spoke death to a fig tree (Matthew 21:19). In all of this he was modeling the power and potential of the Christian faith. Notice, however, that the lack of doubt must be in something called the *heart*. This leads us into our discussion of the subconscious mind.

CHAPTER 7

The Subconscious Mind

The conscious mind is to the soul as the subconscious mind is to the heart. When I speak of the heart I am not referring to the literal organ that pumps blood. I am talking about the non-physical *seat of human intuition*. In the following passage, it is clear that God is looking at something more than a blood-pumping muscle when he references the heart.

"But the LORD said unto Samuel, Look not on his countenance, or on the height of his stature; because I have refused him: for the LORD seeth not as man seeth; for man looketh on the outward appearance, but **the LORD looketh on the heart**" (1 Samuel 16:7).

THE WORD DISCERNS THE HEART

When considering how to understand the heart, it can be difficult. Some have tried to understand it as the spirit. This is unfortunately an incorrect assessment, although the confusion is warranted. To break the power of confusion, we are going to take a brief exploration into the original Hebrew in order to assess the terms from which we translate *soul*, *heart*, and *spirit*. In the Old Testament, the Hebrew word translated heart is *leb*. It is used figuratively for the feelings, the will, and even the intellect; likewise the center of anything. These are elements that are associated with the soul.

The word *leb* is used in contrast to the Hebrew words *nephesh*, *neshamah*, and *ruwach*. All of these words deal with internal elements of the human design. *Ruwach*, while on occasion translated *mind*, has much more to with the spirit realm. Some of its definitions include "wind, breath, mind, and spirit." For instance, God's Holy Spirit is called *Ha Kodesh Ruwach*. *Nephesh* is translated as *mind* on occasion, but is also used for the soul in general. Literally it refers to "a breathing creature" but also has "mind" and "person" as its definitions in addition to "heart." Another Hebrew word that is important is *neshamah*. This is what God breathed into Adam to make him a *nephesh*. It means "breath" or "spirit."

"And the LORD God formed man of the dust of the ground, and breathed into his nostrils the breath [neshamah] of life; and man became a living soul [nephesh]" (Genesis 2:7).

It is not my goal to dive into a verse-by-verse exploration of all of these different terms. My goal is to simply show that there are different terms available to us in the original Hebrew that pertain to the composition of man. *Leb,* most often translated *heart,* is different from all of these yet has definitional characteristics that seem to allude most closely to those that relate to the function of the soul (which we have addressed in the previous chapter). *This is why I understand it as (the lowest) part of the soul, but functioning as the point of transition between things soul and spirit, operating like a gateway between the two.*

Having made this distinction, it remains true that in the heart there exists an overlay of at least part of the spirit. This is brought out in the following passage, in which we learn where true Jews are circumcised according to the New Covenant. They are circumcised "of the heart, in the spirit," which reads in the Greek *kardia en pneuma*. Clearly, there is an overlay of heart and spirit.

"But he is a Jew, which is one inwardly; and circumcision is that **of the heart, in the spirit**, and not in the letter; whose praise is not of men, but of God" (Romans 2:29).

In the New Testament the Greek word translated as *heart* is *kardia*. This word is used figuratively for the thoughts or feelings of the mind and also by analogy the middle. Again, these elements are associated with the soul. This is why I believe that the heart is a component of the soul, which overlays upon at least a portion of the spirit. The biblical revelation of the heart moves us far beyond the conscious mind into an entirely separate realm, which I call the subconscious mind.[12] As we begin to assess the biblical revelation of the heart, this will become inarguably apparent. Let us begin with the following passage.

"For the word of God is quick, and powerful, and sharper than any twoedged sword, piercing even to the dividing asunder of soul and spirit, and of the joints and marrow, and is a discerner of the thoughts and intents of the heart" (Hebrews 4:12).

This particular passage discusses the operation of the word of God in an individual. It is quick, meaning that it quickens, or gives life. The word of God, which is synonymous with the person of Jesus Christ (John 1), brings true and eternal life to us. This eternal life doesn't begin when we die, but the impact is intended to be felt while we yet live. Jesus came to give us life and to give it to us more abundantly (John 10:10). The Bible adds that those who receive an abundance of grace and receive God's gift of righteousness will *reign in life* through Jesus Christ (Romans 5:17).

The word of God is powerful, meaning that it has the power to change and transform lives beyond all logic. It not only gives us wisdom, but also knowledge and understanding. It is empowered by the very Spirit of God to have a transformational effect. The difference between wisdom, knowledge, and understanding can be summarized in the following way:

Knowledge: the possession of the facts of truth

Understanding: the interpretation of truth

Wisdom: the application of truth

The word of God is also sharp. It has the ability to divide what is soul from what is spirit. This doesn't make sense until we understand that the soul and spirit are separate things. Nonetheless, they have a large degree of interaction. Where do the soul and the spirit interact? Their interactions take place in the heart. This is why, while the word of God divides what is soul from what is spirit, it is simultaneously discerning the thoughts and intents of the heart. *The thoughts and intents of the heart are our subconscious operations.*

HEART, SOUL, AND SPIRIT

The heart is a meeting place, gateway, or processing unit between the soul and the spirit. It contains the belief system that resides at the core of the individual; thus, it is best defined as the subconscious mind. This belief system is formed according to information that is presented to the heart from both the spirit and the soul. The spirit puts information about spiritual things into our heart, while the soul (or conscious mind) puts information derived from our life experiences into our heart.

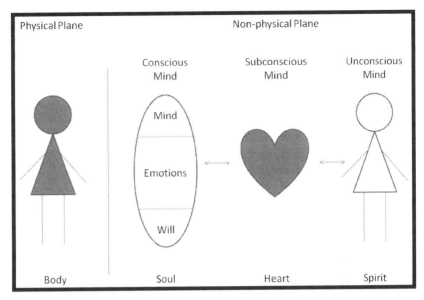

Figure 20

There is a flow of information into the heart and there is a simultaneous flow of information from the heart. This is indicated by the double arrows in the figure. The spirit feeds spiritual information into the heart and the soul feeds carnal information into the heart. In response, the heart sends out information that shapes the activity of both the soul and spirit based upon the belief system that is presently in operation. In this way, whatever the heart is convinced of creates the person's reality—this is what is meant when the Bible says "as he thinks in his heart, so is he."

"For as he thinks in his heart, so is he. As one who reckons, he says to you, eat and drink, yet his heart is not with you [but is grudging the cost]" (Proverbs 23:7 AMPC).

The Bible also declares that the issues of life flow from the heart. This is the same revelation. The words translated as *issues* in the following verse can also be understood as "borders" or "boundaries." The boundary markers of our life flow from or are established by our heart. Whatever thoughts are dominant in our heart will ultimately create the reality we experience. If you have issues, check your heart!

"Keep thy **heart** with all diligence; for out of it are the **issues of life**" (Proverbs 4:23).

Heart and Soul

Regarding its impact on the soul, the heart sends out information that either empowers or inhibits the activities manifesting from the mind, will, and emotions. For instance, if a person's belief system contains the belief that they will never be wealthy, then all mental, willful, and emotional activity that could lead to wealth will be stunted by the heart. If a person's belief system contains the belief that God doesn't love him or her, then all mental, willful, and emotional activity towards attending a church, Bible study, or prayer meeting will be stifled by the heart.

I am amazed sometimes at how much money people will invest to go to various workshops and conferences. They will attend self-help conferences, Christian conferences, marketing conferences, motivational conferences, and so forth. The purpose, of course, is to find more effective ways to live life and conduct business. More amazing than what people will spend is what people will incorporate. My observation is that most people will incorporate little, if any, of what they pay to learn. They feel good about hearing what they heard and settle for that. Why would a person do something so ridiculous after investing so much? The fact of the matter is that this is a heart issue. The information isn't changing their heart, and so their heart actually stifles their ability to incorporate the change.

Heart and Spirit

Regarding its impact on the spirit, if unbelief is present in a person's heart, it will circumvent the power of faith. It will literally inhibit a person's ability to receive anything from God and absolutely prohibit them from walking out their authority in Christ. This is why the heart can be deceitful above all things and desperately wicked. In the original Hebrew, this word translated as *desperately wicked* speaks to the frail, woeful, and melancholy nature the human heart can exhibit.

"The heart is deceitful above all things, and desperately wicked: who can know it?" (Jeremiah 17:9).

Truly understanding the heart requires us to understand how the spirit and the soul interact with it. Regarding the spiritual activity of a Christian, when we have been born again, the Holy Spirit enters into and proceeds to live in our spirit (Ephesians 1:13). This is why the Bible says, "He that is joined to the Lord is one spirit with him" (1 Corinthians 6:17). The presence of the Holy Spirit in our spirit allows the Holy Spirit to put information directly into our heart. This means that the Bible isn't intended to be the *only* source of information that God is giving to us. The Holy Spirit will personally teach us, using the Bible to confirm the things which are truly of him.

"But the Comforter, which is the Holy Ghost, whom the Father will send in my name, he shall teach you all things, and bring all things to your remembrance, whatsoever I have said unto you" (John 14:26).

SALVATION OF THE HEART

A false assumption made by many Christians is the thought that if a person is saved, Jesus is automatically dwelling in that person's heart. The problem is that since the heart hasn't been understood, flawed interpretations have resulted. While all Christians *should* have Jesus dwelling in their hearts, what this really means is that their subconscious has been overridden by the thoughts and person of Jesus Christ. This is slightly different than being made one with the Spirit of God (1 Corinthians 6:17), since we are talking about activity occurring on two separate levels of our existence. The heart is not the spirit, and the spirit is not the heart. There is simply a degree of overlap between the two.

At new birth it is our spirit that is reborn. From this point it is necessary for us to attain (and maintain) an abiding state that allows Jesus to actively dwell in our heart. The salvation of the spirit is not necessarily synonymous with this activity. During radical conversions, the two events can occur simultaneously; however, it is important to understand that this isn't always the case, and even when it is, it must be maintained. It is possible to go through a season of life where our subconscious is ruled by the ideologies and perspectives of Jesus, only to backslide later.

This was clearly the case with the Church of Laodicea, which was declared lukewarm by Jesus (Revelation 3:16). The Church didn't start off lukewarm, they *became* lukewarm. They backslid until they were neither hot nor cold. Even the Church of Ephesus was said to have lost its first love (Revelation 2:4). This is why Paul felt compelled to pray for *Christians* in his epistle to the Ephesians that Christ would dwell in their hearts by faith. He wasn't praying for the lost, he was praying for Christians. Moreover, he differentiated between the work of the Holy Spirit in their spirits (inner man) and the activity of Christ dwelling in their hearts. It requires a work to be done in our spirit in order for Christ to dwell in our hearts by faith.

"For this cause I bow my knees unto the Father of our Lord Jesus Christ [the prayer begins]..._That he would grant you, according to the riches of his glory, to [1] **be strengthened with might by his Spirit in the inner man**. [2] **That Christ may dwell in your hearts by faith**" (Ephesians 3:14, 16–17a).

As a matter of fact, Christ dwelling in our hearts by faith appears to be a prerequisite to comprehending the love, and therefore the very nature, of God. If a Christian has the Holy Spirit, but has pushed Christ out of their subconscious in favor of deception, sin, and self-defeating ideologies, they are subverting the power of God in their own lives. They literally cripple the ability of God to be at work in and through them because they have backslidden. This happens to people for various reasons. It may be because of unfortunate situations that have left them feeling betrayed by God. It may be because of unanswered questions, severe spiritual attacks, or any other number of strategies employed by the enemy to destroy Christians. Whatever the cause, we must accept that God's will is for Jesus to dwell in our hearts by faith—period.

It is also common to find people who never grow to the point where they allow Christ to overhaul their subconscious. Many Christians never go deep enough with God to get to this place, yet they wonder why they find it hard to encounter the power, presence, majesty, and love that their Creator has for them. Allowing Christ to dwell in our subconscious is the prerequisite to *experiencing* the love of God as a part of our Christian lifestyle. *Choosing to believe* that God loves us and *tangibly experiencing* his love are two separate things. We are to experientially know the love of Christ, and ultimately be filled with all the fullness of God.

"That Christ may dwell in your hearts by faith; that ye, being rooted and grounded in love, May be able to comprehend with all saints what is the breadth, and length, and depth, and height; And to know the love of

Christ, which passeth knowledge, that ye might be filled with all the fulness of God" (Ephesians 3:17–19).

A Perceived Contradiction of Terms

There is a verse in Scripture that has confused many regarding this issue. As a matter of fact, this verse has been one of the primary reasons people have failed to distinguish the difference between the heart and the spirit.

"[He has also appropriated and acknowledged us as His by] putting His seal upon us and giving us His [Holy] Spirit in our hearts as the security deposit *and* guarantee [of the fulfillment of His promise]" (2 Corinthians 1:22 AMPC).

This verse is clear that the Holy Spirit has been given to us in our hearts. This occurs as God puts a seal upon us. The placing of this seal unto the day of redemption (as a proof of purchase) is echoed in Ephesians 1:13 and Ephesians 4:30. How can it be that Christ doesn't automatically dwell in the heart of the believer if this verse clearly says that God has given us the Holy Spirit in our hearts? In response to this question, many have simply settled for believing that the heart is the spirit. The problem is that passages like Ephesians 3:16–17 are not resolved by this approach. Now that the problem has been identified and articulated, how can we understand 2 Corinthians 1:22 in light of the whole of Scripture?

First, there are two separate works in view. The first is the seal of God, which is placed on our spirit. This occurs when the Holy Spirit becomes one with our spirit (1 Corinthians 6:17). This work is separated from the work that occurs in our heart by the word *and*. It is written, "(1) putting his seal upon us **and** (2) giving us his [Holy] Spirit in our hearts."

Second, at salvation we receive a new heart, and with it comes the Holy Spirit. We cannot receive this new heart without him. It is a heart that will allow the Holy Spirit to write upon it (2 Corinthians 3:3). The problem is that through bad decisions, poor discipleship, and sin, the presence of God and his work in the heart of a believer can be pushed out—literally. It requires a purposeful walk of repentance and intimacy with God to experience the perpetual presence of God in our hearts. This understanding creates a balance between the many Scriptures that we have employed to decipher this issue.

This is also why Paul says that we should not grieve the Holy Spirit. Immediately after telling us not to grieve the Holy Spirit, he tells us exactly how we grieve him. When we grieve the Holy Spirit with our sin and disobedience, we are pushing the influence of God out of our subconscious. This is why when we are in sin we feel so distant from God. This is why when we are in sin it can be so difficult to hear from God. This is why when we are in sin we can feel as though God has left us. While he hasn't left us, we have effectively pushed him out of our subconscious realm and distanced ourselves from his influence by a whole order of magnitude.

"And do not grieve the Holy Spirit of God [do not offend or vex or sadden Him], by Whom you were sealed (marked, branded as God's own, secured) for the day of redemption (of final deliverance through Christ from evil and the consequences of sin). Let all bitterness and indignation and wrath (passion, rage, bad temper) and resentment (anger, animosity) and quarreling (brawling, clamor, contention) and slander (evil-speaking, abusive or blasphemous language) be banished from you, with all malice (spite, ill will, or baseness of any kind)" (Ephesians 4:30–31 AMPC).

A New Heart

What still amazes me is that God not only puts the Holy Spirit in our spirit, but he also puts a new heart within us. God makes provision for us to have everything we need to embrace the totality of all that he has purchased for us. We don't earn a new heart, the Bible says we are simply given one. This heart is capable of accommodating Jesus as its abiding resident. Furthermore, since we know that becoming a Christian does not require an organ transplant, we have further confirmation that when the Bible references the heart, it is referring to the realm of the subconscious mind (existing on the non-physical plane). Speaking of his forthcoming work regarding the nation of Israel, God speaks the following.

"I will give them an undivided heart and put a new spirit in them; I will remove from them their heart of stone and give them a heart of flesh. Then they will follow my decrees and be careful to keep my laws. They will be my people, and I will be their God" (Ezekiel 11:19–20).

While I do not believe that God has done away with plans for genetic Israel (as replacement theology would argue), I acknowledge that the Church has become spiritual Israel (Romans 2:29, Ephesians 2:11-14). Before we come to Jesus we have a divided heart. God promises to give us an undivided heart and to put a new Spirit in us. This new Spirit is his Holy Spirit, which fuses with our spirit and causes us to be reborn spiritually. God also promises to remove the heart of stone and give us a heart of flesh. In other words, God promises to reformat the heart of the Christian so that he or she can receive and process heavenly information. God makes it possible for our heart (meaning our subconscious) to be written on by the Spirit of the Living God.

"Forasmuch as ye are manifestly declared to be the epistle of Christ ministered by us, written not with ink, but with the Spirit of the living God; not in tables of stone, but in fleshy tables of the heart" (2 Corinthians 3:3).

The easiest way to understand this is by using a model. There are several platforms for computers, but the most common are Macintosh and PC. For our example, pretend that the PC represents the heart of stone and the Macintosh represents the heart of flesh. In most cases, what will work on a PC will not work on a Macintosh, and vice versa. If I have a PC, but I want to run a Macintosh program, I have to get a new computer. I cannot install the Macintosh program onto the PC and expect it to work right. In the same way, the Spirit of God must write into a heart of flesh given to us by God. If the Spirit of God tries to write in the divided heart of stone it will not work. This is just like trying to run a Macintosh program on a PC. Understanding this, God doesn't just give us the "Macintosh software." He also gives us the "Macintosh computer" to go with it. In other words, not only does God give us his Spirit, but he prepares our subconscious to interact with his Spirit. This combination allows us to operate according to the heavenly paradigms that he is inscribing into us.

Moreover, just like we install programs on a computer, we install belief systems into our heart. Just like we uninstall programs on a computer, we must uninstall belief systems systematically. *Our belief systems are "installed" as a result of our dominant source(s) of information. This information is presented from both the soul and the spirit for processing by the heart.*

Once a belief system is installed, it doesn't just change on the flip of a dime. This is because subconscious thoughts exist beneath the realm of direct conscious manipulation. If I say the words *pink elephant*, I can get your conscious mind to immediately think about pink elephants. However, by saying those words I have in no way impacted your belief system. I have not changed your subconscious mind. Changing the subconscious mind is akin to installing and uninstalling programs.

Programming the Subconscious

Since changing the subconscious mind is so much like installing and uninstalling programs on a computer, it can be viewed as "programming." The question is: how do we "program" the subconscious? The three main ways to program the subconscious are as follows:

1. Revelation
2. Repetition
3. Trauma

Revelation comes from the spirit realm, and ideally comes from God. It is knowledge extracted from the spirit realm that goes directly into our hearts. Although revelation does not always have God as its source (there are revelations into evil things), this seems to be the method of subconscious programming that God favors. This is why salvation involves having the Holy Spirit inside of us, so that we gain unlimited access to revelation from God.

Revelation does not require that our conscious mind fully understand the issue. The impact of revelation is instantaneous, and often transcends the power of natural logic. Revelation rewires our belief system first, and impacts our conscious mind second. When it comes from God it is extremely positive in nature. According to the following verse, the spirit of wisdom and revelation leads to the opening of the eyes of our understanding.

"That the God of our Lord Jesus Christ, the Father of glory, may give unto you the spirit of wisdom and revelation in the knowledge of him: **The eyes of your understanding** being enlightened; that ye may know what is the hope of his calling, and what the riches of the glory of his inheritance in the saints" (Ephesians 1:17–18).

The "eyes of our understanding" in this case means the eyes of our heart, as the Amplified Bible so accurately points out. Revelation awakens the heart (or subconscious mind) to God's programming.

"[For I always pray to] the God of our Lord Jesus Christ, the Father of glory, that He may grant you a spirit of wisdom and revelation [of insight into mysteries and secrets] in the [deep and intimate] knowledge of Him, By having **the eyes of your heart** flooded with light, so that you can know and understand the hope to which He has called you, and how rich is His glorious inheritance in the saints (His set-apart ones)" (Ephesians 1:17–18 AMPC).

After revelation comes repetition. For a majority of people, repetition is the primary way through which the heart gets programmed. It involves repetitive bombardment of information. When the mind gets used to processing a certain type of information, there comes a point when any information that seems contradictory appears ludicrous. Once upon a time, people believed that smoking was a healthy lifestyle choice. This was due to advertising campaigns in which doctors were portrayed as endorsing cigarettes. When information began to emerge that challenged this thought, people didn't immediately buy into it. Could smoking really have negative effects on health? It wasn't that the evidence didn't make sense. It was that this information contradicted the heart belief established by the *repetitive* presentation of information explaining that "physicians endorse smoking."

Repetition does not manifest from the spirit but from the natural. The experiences, education, and information we take in during our day-to-day lives will dictate this form of programming. As they say, *"garbage in, garbage out."* It is impossible to repeatedly subject a person to degradation, evil, and filth and expect that they'll walk away in great moral shape. This is why the media and entertainment we subject ourselves to must be carefully judged. By having people bombarded with violence, revenge, rape, pornography, gossip, and filthy language, a society can be brought to its knees in sin.

"He that walketh righteously, and speaketh uprightly; he that despiseth the gain of oppressions, that shaketh his hands from holding of bribes, **that stoppeth his ears from hearing of blood, and shutteth his eyes from seeing evil; He shall dwell on high**: his place of defence shall be the munitions of rocks: bread shall be given him; his waters shall be sure" (Isaiah 33:15–16).

Repetition can be utilized for both good and bad. An example of using it for good takes us back to the last chapter. In it we discussed the importance of renewing the mind. Renewing our conscious mind according to the word of God is an extremely positive use of repetition. By repeatedly subjecting ourselves to God's word, we are actually programming our belief system, even when we aren't necessarily getting direct revelation. Renewing our mind is an indispensable practice in the Christian faith.

An example of using repetition for evil agendas includes brainwashing people. It includes putting thousands and thousands of sexual references and innuendos into entertainment. It includes putting inappropriate images on every billboard, every magazine stand, and in every place print advertisements can be found. It includes emotionally abusing people by telling them over and over again that they are useless, incapable, unworthy, and hopeless. The list of negative uses of repetition could seemingly go on forever.

The third main way to program the heart is with trauma. Trauma is the worst way to program a belief system because it requires a terrible situation. For example, people who grow up in abusive situations often have belief systems that have been programmed and characterized by the trauma they have endured. War is also a clear route through which individuals are negatively impacted by trauma. Trauma can come emotionally, sexually, spiritually, or physically, but regardless of how it comes, it leaves the belief system of a person scarred. As a matter of fact, when trauma is bad enough it will lead to Dissociative Identity Disorder (DID), which results in the presence of multiple personalities within a person's subconscious. This will often go hand-in-hand with Satanic Ritual Abuse (SRA).

Until sufficient inner healing has taken place within an individual, it is often difficult or nearly impossible for that person to break free of the resulting belief system. Belief systems that are programmed via trauma are more easily manipulated by the devil, and rarely allow the individual to rise to their true potential.

"Be sober, be vigilant; because your adversary the devil, as a roaring lion, walketh about, seeking whom he may devour" (1 Peter 5:8).

Trauma leads to a broken heart. It leads to an individual who is shattered. This is why Jesus Christ has come to bind up the brokenhearted. This is why Jesus Christ is the ultimate solution to the programming that is established in an individual's life due to severe trauma.

"He healeth the broken in heart, and bindeth up their wounds" (Psalm 147:3).

"The Spirit of the Lord God is upon me; because the Lord hath anointed me to preach good tidings unto the meek; he hath sent me to bind up the brokenhearted, to proclaim liberty to the captives, and the opening of the prison to them that are bound" (Isaiah 61:1).

A Perfect Heart

It may come as a surprise to many people that while a sinless life is unrealistic on this side of eternity, it is possible to achieve a perfect heart. What is a perfect heart? It is a subconscious fully persuaded to fulfill the purposes of God. It is a subconscious that is fully given over to God, even in the midst of imperfect circumstances. As we will see, it doesn't require a sinless life to have a perfect heart. Even in all of his flaws, King David was spoken of as having a perfect heart. While we won't spend much time on this subject, the following are some verses for your consideration.

"**Let your heart therefore be perfect** with the Lord our God, to walk in his statutes, and to keep his commandments, as at this day" (1 Kings 8:61).

"And he walked in all the sins of his father, which he had done before him: and **his heart was not perfect with the Lord his God, as the heart of David** his father" (1 Kings 15:3).

"But the high places were not removed: nevertheless **Asa's heart was perfect** with the Lord all his days" (1 Kings 15:14).

"All these men of war, that could keep rank, **came with a perfect heart** to Hebron, to make David king over all Israel: and all the rest also of Israel were of one heart to make David king" (1 Chronicles 12:38).

From Subconscious to Unconscious

The subconscious mind is a realm of human nature that desperately needs to be understood. Faith is a matter of the heart. The effectiveness of faith, which is the currency of heaven, depends entirely upon the subconscious. Furthermore, a majority of what manifests in our lives is tied to the belief systems of our heart. As we will discuss later, even our interaction with parallel dimensions is most likely tied to the activity of our hearts. It is *absolutely essential* that the subconscious mind be understood.

However, stopping at the subconscious mind leaves us with an over-simplification regarding our nature. The unconscious mind must be understood as well. The fact of the matter is that our understanding of higher dimensions cannot continue apart from understanding the unconscious mind. This subject will project our journey into the realm of the spirit.

CHAPTER 8

The Unconscious Mind

Our spirit, which contains our unconscious mind, remains for the most part poorly understood, at best. Why is this true? As we will soon come to understand, our spirit has a trans-dimensional nature. Trying to explain this without context has proven to be excessively difficult for many people. When I use the term *trans-dimensional*, I am intending to communicate that our spirit is operating on multiple dimensional planes simultaneously.

Before getting into the trans-dimensional nature of the spirit, let us first discover why the spirit is best understood as the unconscious mind. To be *unconscious* basically means "to lack any form of awareness." Therefore, an unconscious mind would be a mind processing thoughts and information that we lack any form of awareness about. The average person has absolutely no awareness of spiritual things. Many people do not so much as know that they have a "spirit." Imagine if I were to ask the average person on the street, "How is your spirit today?" I would probably get very awkward responses. They may think that by "spirit" I am simply implying "mood," or they may just look at me sideways. People are unconscious regarding what their spirit is experiencing.

Spiritual Experiences

Through various techniques, it is possible for people to make themselves aware of spiritual things. Certain types of (non-biblical) meditations, rituals, and hallucinatory drugs can cause this to happen. However, without Christ, it can be detrimental for people to open themselves up to spiritual things. The reason is because there are many evil spirits waiting for the opportunity to destroy the lives of people. When doors are opened up to them, via non-biblical spirituality, it will allow these evil spirits to bring the individual under increasingly severe oppression, torment, and control.

With Jesus it is possible to enjoy radical spiritual experiences in the safety of the hands of the Living God. What is interesting is that in spite of this, many people who have Christ are *not* open to spiritual things. This is truly unfortunate. As this book progresses, it is my prayer that you as the reader will find the spirit realm and the spiritual benefits of Jesus Christ becoming more real to you. It is my prayer that you will allow him to take your relationship with him to levels you did not formerly know existed.

The Location of the Christian Spirit

Earlier in this work I pointed out the following Scripture. It reveals to us the location of our spirit when we have obtained salvation through Jesus Christ.

"And hath raised us up together, and made us sit together in heavenly places in Christ Jesus" (Ephesians 2:6).

This passage explains that Christians have been elevated together into something called "heavenly places." This means that prior to receiving Jesus, our spirit was on a lower plane; and that upon receiving him, our spirit was "raised up" to a higher plane. It is a simple fact that Christians do not have regular revelation regarding their activity in these places. We may at times feel the presence of God, but for most Christians to describe heavenly places, they will have to pull out their Bible and begin reading. I want to be clear that there is nothing wrong with this. The point is that we need to understand that this verse is true, regardless of whether it feels true or not. The reason we don't consciously experience these heavenly places (where we presently are) is because the experience is being processed by our unconscious mind.

We have already described "heavenly places" as locations found in the spirit realm that are scattered across different dimensions. We also learned that the dimensions are divided between three heavens. We defined the first heaven as all that is contained by earth's atmosphere, and the second heaven as the spirit realm. We defined the third heaven as the realm in which God dwells. We conceptualized the second heaven as beginning at the division between the third and fourth dimensions. We conceptualized the third heaven as beginning at the division between the seventh and eighth dimensions.

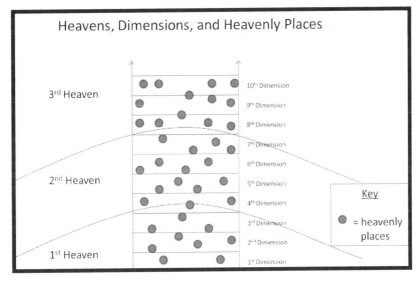

Figure 21

Ephesians 2:6 explains that we are raised into heavenly places "in Christ"—meaning the heavenly places found in the third heaven (or the realm of God). In other words, this requires that our spirit be in operation on a very high spiritual plane. Moreover, it means that the environment taking place around our spirit at any given time incorporates many dimensions, making the environment virtually impossible to describe with three-dimensional concepts. We must come to terms with the fact that our spirit is able to interact with an environment that is far beyond our ability to conceptualize. *We must also accept that, in effect, the Christian actually takes heaven with him or her wherever they go.* In order to be involved in all of this activity, our spirit uses spiritual senses.

SPIRITUAL SENSES

Senses are required to engage the natural world, just like senses are required to engage the spirit world. Most of us are familiar with the famous "five senses." These senses are possessed by the majority of people. They are so vital that when one of them is eliminated, we consider that person "disabled." The five senses are touch, sight, hearing, taste, and smell. The interesting thing is that just like our body, our spirit also has these same senses. When we read about them in the Bible, we often write it off as allegory. However, this couldn't be further from the truth. These passages simply explain the ability of our spirit to engage the spirit realm. They show us the kind of information our unconscious mind is actively processing.

And he shewed me Joshua the high priest standing before the angel of the Lord, and Satan standing at his right hand to resist him. And the Lord said unto Satan, The Lord rebuke thee, O Satan; even the Lord that hath chosen Jerusalem rebuke thee: is not this a brand plucked out of the fire? Now Joshua was clothed with filthy garments, and stood before the angel. And he answered and spake unto those that stood before him, saying, Take away the filthy garments from him. And unto him he said, Behold, I have caused thine iniquity to pass from thee, and I will clothe thee with change of raiment. And I said, Let them set a fair mitre upon his head. So they set a fair mitre upon his head, and clothed him with garments. And the angel of the Lord stood by.

(Zechariah 3:1–5)

Zechariah was a prophet appointed to Israel after the conclusion of the seventy-year captivity. In this scene, Zechariah had a heavenly vision and saw Joshua the high priest (not the Joshua of the Book of Joshua) standing before the Lord. Joshua was the appointed high priest of that day. In the Book of Zechariah, Joshua the high priest and Zerubbabel the governor were the "two witnesses," otherwise referenced as the two olive trees, of that generation (Zechariah 4).

This event occurred in the spirit realm and on a higher dimension. It was centered on the judgment of God concerning the spirit of Joshua. Zechariah was made privy to a spiritual event that was taking place. Zechariah was permitted to see the activity occurring around Joshua's spirit. The spirit of Joshua was wearing filthy garments and then experienced a change of raiment right before the throne of God! A mitre was even set upon his spirit's head. The ability for our spirit to "wear clothing" implies **TOUCH**. The spiritual clothes touched and covered his spirit.

This isn't the only revelation that spirits have the sense of touch. We see that angels, which are spirits (Psalm 104:4), touch people (Daniel 9:21), hold objects like trumpets (Revelation 8:2) and swords (Numbers 22:23), and write in books (Malachi 3:16). If angelic spirits can touch spiritual objects to do these things, why would our spirits be any different?

"For this people's heart is waxed gross, and their ears are dull of hearing, and their eyes they have closed; lest at any time they should see with their eyes and hear with their ears, and should understand with their heart, and should be converted, and I should heal them" (Matthew 13:15).

In this passage, Jesus was addressing his disciples. He had just finished speaking to a multitude of people who had gathered to hear him talk. *Thousands of people had literally just seen and heard Jesus.* Were they all deaf and blind? No. They could see and hear him just fine (in the natural). The issue Jesus addressed was their ability to hear and see spiritually. He was talking about their spirits. The human spirit has the ability to **HEAR** and **SEE**.

"And have tasted the good word of God, and the powers of the world to come" (Hebrews 6:5).

The word of God is compared to food on numerous occasions in the Bible. In one passage it is explained that babes in Christ should earnestly desire the milk of the Word (1 Peter 2:2). These are to be understood as the basic principles of the faith. There is also the meat of the Word (Hebrews 5:12, 14), which belongs to mature believers. This may seem like it should be interpreted as allegory, but that would be an oversimplification. Our spirit is *literally* fed by the word of God. What do you think the bread of life is (John 6:38)? Moreover, if we had a greater degree of access to our unconscious mind, we would actually comprehend the **TASTE** of that word.

"O taste and see that the Lord is good: blessed is the man that trusteth in him" (Psalm 34:8).

Not only is our spirit man able to taste the word of God, we are also able to taste and see his goodness. In this verse, we again find a reference to the senses possessed by our human spirits. This is not just an allegory. This is a literal explanation of how we are to engage God with our spiritual senses.

"But I have all, and abound: I am full, having received of Epaphroditus the things which were sent from you, an odour of a sweet smell, a sacrifice acceptable, wellpleasing to God" (Philippians 4:18).

The Apostle Paul was responsible for planting many churches and writing a large portion of the New Testament. For all of the impact he had, he spent a lot of time paying his own way. He was a tentmaker by trade (Acts 18:3). In his letter to the Philippians, he makes it clear that they were the only church that communicated with him concerning giving and receiving (Philippians 4:15). He went on to say that this monetary gift would not only abound to their heavenly account (Philippians 4:17), but that it had the "odour of a sweet smell." Did they spray these coins with perfume? Probably not. The essence of the passage is that the gift was a sacrifice with a sweet-smelling aroma that was well-pleasing to God. The **SMELL** that he references was the *spiritual* aroma associated with the monetary sacrifice.

From these passages it is absolutely irrefutable that our spirit has senses, just like our body. This is not clear to us primarily because of the nature of our spiritual experiences. The experiences and events associated with the use of our spiritual senses are often hidden from our conscious mind and remain unconscious processes. However, this doesn't make them any less real. Our spirit has daily interactions with spiritual environments, spiritual beings, and spiritual objects.

REGARDING TIME

Our spirit is interacting with a dimension that is not bound by time. The reason this is true is because time exists as a property, or function, of the three-dimensional space to which our physical bodies are bound. Time is considered a temporal dimension (meaning a way to measure physical change). Above the three-dimensional plane, the importance and power of time diminishes. God does not experience time like we do, and neither does the realm in which he exists. As a matter of fact, quantum theory has even identified something called "time loops" involving the interaction between a particle and its antiparticle.[13] In other words, time is not as standard or concrete as has long been believed. As far as our existence in God's realm is concerned, time is a very small consideration. The Bible speaks to this with the following Scripture.

"But, beloved, be not ignorant of this one thing, that one day is with the Lord as a thousand years, and a thousand years as one day" (2 Peter 3:8).

We have established that when we are Christian, our spirit is present in heavenly places. However, our spirit is *also* present in our body, which *is* bound by time. This creates an interesting dichotomy in that, while we are not spiritually bound by time, we are most certainly physically bound by time. Our spirit participates in time along with our body. As we meditate on how an entity (our spirit) can exist both "inside of time" and "outside of time," we realize that it would be very difficult for our mind to understand and conceptualize this experience. Nonetheless, at the core of the human condition there abides a *knowing*. This *knowing* speaks that we were created for more than just our temporary existence on this planet. A few try to ignore this knowing, but history bears the record of human inquisitiveness regarding what to expect in the "after-life." We are born as an eternal spirit occupying a mortal body. After the body dies, eternity awaits us.

"He has made everything beautiful in its time. He also has planted eternity in men's hearts and minds [a divinely implanted sense of a purpose working through the ages which nothing under the sun but God alone can satisfy], yet so that men cannot find out what God has done from the beginning to the end" (Ecclesiastes 3:11 AMPC).

The Spirit is Above the Flesh

We have an existence that is much more complex and sophisticated than even the ultra-complex cellular and molecular structure of our flesh and bones. We are both spirit and flesh, with the spirit being above the flesh. This is why spiritual things like the word of God have the power to impact even the molecular structure of our existence. The spirit is designed to be the point of origin for all things that manifest in the natural. This is why the word of God can pierce even to the dividing asunder of the joints and marrow. As the Holy Spirit once explained to me, "Beneath the sub-molecular realm lies the spirit realm."

"For the word of God is quick, and powerful, and sharper than any twoedged sword, piercing even to the dividing asunder of soul and spirit, and of the **joints and marrow**, and is a discerner of the thoughts and intents of the heart" (Hebrews 4:12).

It is interesting to note that when we get to the sub-molecular realm, particles with very strange behaviors have been observed. This includes tachyons, which are subatomic particle that move at speeds faster than light. When observed, they appear to be moving backwards in time.[14]

Another interesting discovery is that when tardyons, which are particles that move slower than the speed of light, are accelerated, things change. Think of a gun and a target. When tardyons are moving slow relative to light speed, it is like a person shooting a gun. The bullet will travel a distance, and a short time later explode a target (cause precedes effect). As these particles (or anything, really) accelerate to half the speed of light, it is like a person shooting a gun and the target exploding simultaneously (cause equals effect). As tardyons approach light speed, things change again, and it is like a target exploding with a bullet traveling back into the gun, with the gun subsequently loading itself (effect precedes cause).[15]

I like to think that since God is Light (1 John 1:5), as we approach him, the treasures of his realm overtake our time-space experience and replace our reality! In other words, in the kingdom of God, "effect precedes cause." The provisions established by the finished work of Jesus Christ precede our need. As a matter of fact, even the works we walk out as we respond to Jesus with faith and obedience are established in a past-tense framework. This can be highly confusing until we introduce higher concepts of dimensionality. The works that we are appointed to walk in are prepared "beforehand." We pull them into manifestation from the realm of God, which is a place where they have already been established outside of time! This is deep food for thought.

"For we are God's [own] handiwork (His workmanship), recreated in Christ Jesus, [born anew] **that we may do those good works which God predestined (planned beforehand) for us** [taking paths which He prepared ahead of time], that we should walk in them [living the good life which He prearranged and made ready for us to live]" (Ephesians 2:10 AMPC).

In other words, if God tells you to start a business, then from a Scriptural standpoint that business has already been built. It is already established. It is already profitable. It is already producing resources that can be leveraged to expand the influence of the kingdom of God in the earth. You simply need to connect the physical realm with what God has already prepared. Heaven and earth are out of alignment, and it is our job to agree with God and bring heaven and earth into alignment. This is done through faith, obedience, prayer, fasting, and other biblically outlined responses to God. Jesus told us to pray that God's will would be done on earth as it is in heaven for a reason (Matthew 6:10).

When we learn to come in contact with God and his realm, his realities will overtake our experiences. The closer we get to God and the greater our revelation of the kingdom becomes, the more we will move out of a "cause precedes effect" lifestyle and into an "effect precedes cause" lifestyle. We will walk in works that were finished from the foundation of the world (Hebrews 4:3). You may have cancer today, but God can interrupt your situation and replace it with healing and restoration miraculously.

"And his fame went throughout all Syria: and they brought unto him all sick people that were taken with divers diseases and torments, and those which were possessed with devils, and those which were lunatick, and those that had the palsy; and he healed them" (Matthew 4:24).

THE THRONE OF GRACE

When we understand that we have a trans-dimensional nature, it helps to understand quite a bit of the Bible that is usually written off as illusory, or even symbolic. Once we begin to realize that the Bible takes into account the existence of higher dimensions, parallel dimensions, and the activities that take place therein, we realize that much of what we think is allegory (particularly in the Old Testament) is actually speaking to spiritual realities. In the New Testament, one such passage is as follows.

"Let us therefore come boldly unto the throne of grace, that we may obtain mercy, and find grace to help in time of need" (Hebrews 4:16).

In considering this passage, most would agree that we come to the throne of grace in prayer. The question is: How? I cannot walk into my garage, or the local church building, and find the throne of grace. While many Christians would dodge this question with an answer like "*only by the grace of God* can we come before the throne of grace," this question does have a *literal* answer. We come before the throne of grace *in spirit*—literally. The throne room of God happens to exist as a heavenly place within the third heaven. As a Christian, we gain access to this place, and because of the trans-dimensional nature of our spirit, we can literally go to this place when we engage in prayer here on earth.

WALKING BY FAITH

The important lesson to take away is that our unconscious mind is responsible for processing all trans-dimensional information. This is why Christianity requires that we walk by faith and not by sight (2 Corinthians 5:7). A large reason for this is that we don't have direct access to the spectacular experiences being processed by our unconscious mind. For this reason, we simply have to choose to believe that these things are true. The powerful part is that as our subconscious becomes convinced of these facts, they begin to overtake our *experience* in life because as we think in our heart, so will we be. This is why the Holy Spirit is continually trying to feed spiritual information into our heart.

"For as he thinketh in his heart, so is he..." (Proverbs 23:7).

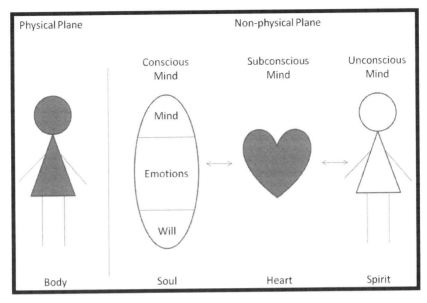

Figure 22

This helps us understand God's wisdom in telling us to trust in him with all of our heart (subconscious) and lean not to our own understanding (Proverbs 3:5). God wants the Christian to operate according to all that is going on in the spirit realm. How small does an unpaid bill become when we consider that we are presently in the company of angels, heavenly realms, and surrounded by the infinite resources of the dimensions of God? When we begin to live and act like this is true, incredible things will take place. As a matter of fact, the Bible speaks directly to the blessings of the heavenly places with the following Scripture.

"Blessed be the God and Father of our Lord Jesus Christ, who hath blessed us with all spiritual blessings **in heavenly places in Christ**" (Ephesians 1:3).

REVISITING ZECHARIAH'S HEAVENLY VISION

Earlier in this chapter, we discussed one of Zechariah's visions. In it he was shown Joshua, the high priest, standing before the throne of God and receiving a change of raiment. I used this to illustrate the fact that the human spirit exhibits the sense of touch. However, just like an onion is peeled back to reveal layer after layer, so it is with this passage. There remains an even deeper and more profound revelation that awaits us. It is the revelation that our spirits are involved in heavenly transactions (and events) that occur *while* we are alive on earth. To preface this discussion, we will revisit this incredible passage of Scripture. This time, we'll look at the Amplified version.

> Then [the guiding angel] showed me Joshua the high priest standing before the Angel of the Lord, and Satan standing at Joshua's right hand to be his adversary and to accuse him. And the Lord said to Satan, The Lord rebuke you, O Satan! Even the Lord, Who [now and habitually] chooses Jerusalem, rebuke you! Is not this [returned captive Joshua] a brand plucked out of the fire? Now Joshua was clothed with filthy garments and was standing before the Angel [of the Lord]. And He spoke to those who stood before Him, saying, Take away the filthy garments from him. And He said to [Joshua], Behold, I have caused your iniquity to pass from you, and I will clothe you with rich apparel. And I [Zechariah] said, Let them put a clean turban on his head. So they put a clean turban on his head and clothed him with [rich] garments. And the Angel of the Lord stood by.
>
> (Zechariah 3:1–5 AMPC)

Only once we realize that this passage deals with Joshua the high priest (and not Joshua of the Book of Joshua) can we embrace the weight of what we are actually being told. This passage is detailing that, while Joshua and Zechariah were both physically alive, Joshua and Zechariah were simultaneously called before the throne of God in the spirit. Joshua was given a change in spiritual clothing, and a turban (or crown) was set upon his head at Zechariah's request. Zechariah's prayer, in the spirit, was answered in real time. Imagine that! God didn't tell them to give Joshua a turban (or crown); Zechariah made the petition and it was granted. All of this happened in the spirit realm while their physical bodies were alive on earth.

Some might argue that there is not enough contextual evidence to substantiate what I am claiming here. Specifically, can we really know that Joshua the high priest was actually alive at the time that this heavenly event took place? Our confirmation comes a few chapters later, where Zechariah is instructed to make a physical crown for a very much physically alive high priest named Joshua. Here we see the pattern of spirit first, natural second. The reason God told Zechariah to make a physical crown was to reflect the spiritual reality of Joshua's endowment with a heavenly crown.

"And the word of the Lord came to me, saying, Accept donations and offerings from these [as representatives of the] exiles, from Heldai, from Tobijah, and from Jedaiah, who have come from Babylon; and come the same day and go to the house of Josiah the son of Zephaniah. Yes, take from them silver and gold, **and make crowns and set [one] upon the head of Joshua the son of Jehozadak, the high priest**" (Zechariah 6:9–11 AMPC).

In Zechariah chapter three, the prophet was actually looking at the activity of Joshua's trans-dimensional spirit. Joshua was very much alive while this whole event took place. Joshua's spirit was present for this event in heaven, and was simultaneously present in his body. He may have been sleeping, taking a bath, praying, or cooking some eggs! Who knows? The fact of the matter is that whatever he was doing in the flesh, it was his unconscious mind that was processing this spectacular event. Chances are that he had no comprehension of what Zechariah was permitted to see. Joshua probably knew that something had changed that day, but until Zechariah came and prophetically revealed to him what had occurred in heaven, Joshua would have likely remained in the dark.

The same is true with us. As Christians, our spirits experience all kinds of heavenly events on a daily basis of which we have no knowledge. All of these events and situations are being processed by our unconscious minds, and for the most part, remain hidden from our conscious understanding. Once again, this is why I am explaining to you that the unconscious mind is housed by the spirit man. How many times have you read the Bible or gone to a prayer meeting and felt something change, yet had no idea how exactly to explain it?

I can only imagine the impact of a group of believers that all matured to the degree that they remained continually aware of the activity of their unconscious minds. This would come about as a result of the intimate walk they maintained with the Spirit of God. It would follow that they would literally walk between worlds. They would walk the earth continually aware of their heavenly authority. They would abide in the revelation that all of the provision of heaven remains perpetually at their fingertips. They would walk the earth fully embracing their identity as the sons (and daughters) of God. They would be the most feared men and women in the earth.

I once had an experience in prayer that really brought all of this home for me. As a preface to this testimony, I want to explain how it happened. This did not come about as an out-of-body experience. I didn't ever have to leave my office where I happened to be praying. As a matter of fact, I never lost awareness of the fact that I was still in my office. As this vision began to come to me it was as if my unconscious mind shifted into my consciousness. This was entirely inspired by the Holy Spirit because I wasn't seeking an experience, I was simply seeking God. What I learned would forever change many paradigms for me.

CHAPTER 9

The Heavenly Experience

This particular heavenly experience was radical. I say "this particular" heavenly experience, because this wasn't the only time I have had visions of heavenly things. On this occasion, I was enabled to experience several aspects of heaven while in prayer.

It began as I was going to pray for someone. I was asking God to show me how the enemy had bound a particular person in the realms of the second heaven. At this point in my life I had achieved a limited understanding regarding the importance of second heaven activities. This had led to my peculiar success with spiritual warfare and getting others set free in the name of Jesus. We will talk more about this later in the book. On this occasion, however, instead of showing me elements of second heaven activity, God told me to come up to his heavenly places.

ARRIVING

Suddenly, I was sitting in what appeared to be a room. I was sitting at a table, and on the opposite side of the table was Jesus. Keep in mind that although I was experiencing this as a vision, part of me was still conscious of the fact that I was sitting at my desk. It wasn't quite what some might call an "open vision" or a "trance," but it was no less effective. Jesus proceeded to explain a few things to me. One of the items on his list was that he wanted me to begin doing my warfare differently. Instead of going into the realms of captivity in the second heaven, he ultimately wanted me to be making my commands from the third heaven. We will discuss "realms of captivity" in a later chapter.

As we were sitting at this table, Jesus said that he wanted me to begin to travel here regularly, because I needed to get acquainted with his kingdom in order to preach and teach about it. In other words, he wanted me to get acquainted with the spiritual atmosphere and elements of heaven. As I continued to grow in Christ after this experience, I realized that having heavenly visions was not a requirement to "travel to and get acquainted with" heavenly places. We all can get acquainted with heavenly places because we do it by faith.

I found it incredibly interesting that I was in a room. One would not expect such a thing. However, there is so much to the heavenly dimensions that nothing should take us by surprise. I simply lean not on my own understanding but trust in the verse that says, "I have yet many things to say unto you, *but ye cannot bear them now.* Howbeit when he, the Spirit of truth, is come, he will guide you into all truth: for he shall not speak of himself; but whatsoever he shall hear, that shall he speak: and he will shew you things to come (John 16:12–13)."

It was at this time that I had a revelation that when Jesus seats us in heavenly places, he places us in rooms. Once there it is our responsibility to get up, walk around, explore, and obtain the things from his kingdom that we need in this life. In other words, our spirit is not always in the same location in heaven at all times while we are yet on earth. Going back to my point in the last chapter, our spirit has experiences we often have no idea about.

Exploring

When I walked out of the room, I saw the grass of heaven, the colors, and the perfection. This is particularly difficult to describe because of the nature of my experience. Since I wasn't removed from my body and I still had partial consciousness of my office, some of the vision came as impressions. I was simultaneously aware of spiritual information and natural information. For this reason, while I saw and experienced the atmosphere of the grass, the colors, and the perfection, I wasn't fully engulfed by the experience. I knew what was there; I could sense it. But I didn't fully experience it as I may have if the Holy Spirit had allowed me an out-of-body experience (an experience I have never had, to my knowledge).

In any case, I also saw trees, and they were bearing fruit. I wanted to eat the fruit of the heavenly trees, so I did. My spirit ate of the fruit. Again, the idea that such a thing as spiritual food exists should make perfect sense when we consider that the word of God is referred to as both milk (1 Peter 2:2) and meat (Hebrews 5:14), as referenced in the last chapter. However, the idea of our spirit literally eating is revelatory. The result is spiritual fulfillment. In my case, I did not have a corresponding sensation in my physical mouth that allowed me to understand how the fruit tasted to my spirit. Even if I had, it would have been irrelevant.

Once I had eaten a piece of fruit, Jesus began to show me other rooms. He showed me a room full of treasure, and all I can say is *my oh my*! There was so much treasure stored up in there. I beheld precious metals and jewels piled from the floor to the ceiling. I then understood that in order to get the treasure out of the room, I needed a portal. We will be discussing portals later in this book as well. What I learned was that the size of the portal would correspond to our *purpose* and *faith*. Without a purpose from God, and faith to receive, the treasure cannot be retrieved. I also learned that the biggest treasures are stored up for the largest purposes, namely those dealing with entire nations.

"Ask of Me, and I will give You the nations as Your inheritance, and the uttermost parts of the earth as Your possession" (Psalm 2:8 AMPC).

After looking at this room, I also saw a room full of body parts, organs, and even vitamins and minerals. The organs were not a bloody, gory mess. They were perfect, whole, and shining. These are for the healing and restoration of God's people. I then saw a picture of a person ministering. There were tubes coming from heaven to earth (also to be understood as portals). The person ministering was able to bring through these tubes different needs. The size of the tubes for each type of body part or manifestation was based on the faith present. If there was not enough faith, the tubes were not big enough to transport the body parts and organs from the heavenly storehouse. I understood that most ministers have larger tubes for certain types of manifestations than others. This simply means that they have more faith for certain types of healing or restoration.

"Then touched he their eyes, saying, **According to <u>your faith</u> be it unto you**" (Matthew 9:29).

After seeing this room, I saw a brilliant pool of water. I went over to it and then also into it. I want to make mention that travel in this place was not based on time or distance. While at times movement is similar to how one would walk on earth, translation and flight seemed to be just as valid an option. In any case, I not only went over to the pool, I also went into the pool. There were all types of spirits in it—heavenly spirits. There are many orders and types of angelic spirits, and God has angelic spirits of the waters (Revelation 16:5). I then understood that these were in heaven waiting to be loosed into the seas of the earth to destroy the works of the enemy in underwater places. I will discuss more about why they were there and what this means later in the book. Before leaving the water, I prayed that they would be loosed.

What followed was quite humorous yet sobering at the same time. Jesus showed me a vision of myself dancing around, worshipping and praying in heavenly places—with a *blindfold*! I looked so ridiculous to myself. Who would voluntarily keep a blindfold on in such an amazing and powerful place? I couldn't help but chuckle at the image while simultaneously feeling awfully convicted. The Bible is so clear about where I am and what God has already done for me. Who am I to be so wasteful with it?

"For we who have believed (adhered to and trusted in and relied on God) do enter that rest, in accordance with His declaration that those [who did not believe] should not enter when He said, As I swore in My wrath, They shall not enter My rest; and this He said although **[His] works had been completed *and* prepared [and waiting for all who would believe] from the foundation of the world**" (Hebrews 4:3 AMPC).

Jesus said that I need to engage his realm *on purpose* from now on. I need to keep the blindfold off. The time of acclamation is over. I was made to understand that I need to explore. He said that in this place I will sit at his feet and he would teach me true doctrine. He said there are many things I have never been told and never learned. He explained that it was time for these things to be revealed to me. If you are listening, he is presently speaking the same thing to you. I realized that almost no one explores the heavenly places; they all stay seated in their rooms, totally unaware of where they actually are. It's time for us to get a grip on reality!

I realized that from this place I could open portals to anywhere. What I saw and understood looked like opening doorways to other places and dimensions. Some might explain this phenomenon as wormholes. They are constantly utilized between the higher dimensions of the second and third heavens.

I also began to have an appreciation for the fact that the heavenly realms are so big. The place I found myself exploring was just one section. There was something else that I found highly interesting. When I looked to see who was walking around there was virtually *no one*. I couldn't understand why this was true until the next day.

I continued on to realize that it is in the heavenly places that we "walk with God." It blew my mind when I had the revelation that *this is what Enoch did*. He spent time in heaven spiritually. Eventually God just took him. It appears as though somehow Noah spent time there, too. I wonder if it was during his time there that God told him what to do and what was coming regarding the flood.

"And **Enoch walked with God**: and he was not; for God took him" (Genesis 5:24).

"These are the generations of Noah: Noah was a just man and perfect in his generations, and **Noah walked with God**" (Genesis 6:9).

THE VISION CONTINUES

The next day as I entered into prayer, the vision continued in the same fashion that it had come the previous day. It was revealed to me at this time that the place I began to see and explore was entirely my place, or "mansion in the Father's house" (John 14:2). I then realized that all Christians have a place like this in the third heaven. This explained why there weren't other people walking around. It was under my dominion and appointment.

I then understood that those who would enter into it would be under my spiritual umbrella. However, people who were to be under my spiritual umbrella would be brought via dimensional overlap, so that their resources would travel with them. This occurs because spirits also function as realms. I know that this is difficult to imagine, but bear with me. The things that are unable to be understood now will be revealed in great depth by the Holy Spirit at the right time.

What greatly impacted me was the understanding that the treasure room I saw contained the treasures appointed to *my calling*. How fantastic it is to think that there are millions of Christians who have similar, maybe even larger rooms of treasure in their heavenly places! How rich the body of Christ truly is! Furthermore, the body parts I saw are the ones appointed to *my calling*. The army I saw in the pool is appointed to *my calling*, and for the needs that I will have in doing what I have been called to. All of these things are in my heavenly place. Just imagine what you would find in yours.

I saw two booths in this place as well. I say booths because I don't know how else to describe what I was looking at. One received prayer requests from me for others, and another was for receiving prayer requests from others for me. When these are processed, the heavenly places will align with those of others and create divine appointments through dimensional overlaps. Resources and talents can be merged through this process. I then understood that this is how God brings ministries together. The Bible illustrated this when God commissioned and sent Paul and Barnabas. God created a divine commission involving the overlapping of their heavenly resources by partnering ministries for the advancement of the kingdom (Acts 13:1–2). The more who are joined in unity, the more potential is being pooled for the purposes of God to be manifested in the earth. *This is also intended to be a benefit of marriage*, in that the resources of two are merged when they become "one flesh" (Genesis 2:24).

God also gave me further explanation pertaining to the treasure in the treasure room. When I step out in faith, I am pulling from this storehouse. The way that provision is actually released in the natural has no relevance. It can come from anywhere as we receive it by faith. It can come from a job promotion, an unforeseen opportunity, an unexpected inheritance, or a random blessing. There can even be some occasions when God will manifest riches out of thin air to prove his ability. It is not beyond

God's ability to materialize a pile of gold or jewels out of nothing, and there have been several reports of this.[16,17] However, what God truly wants is for us to learn to live like it's there without seeing it.

Faith is the currency of heaven. It is no different for the room of riches than for the room of body parts. God is not going to materialize a liver in my office. He will materialize it into the body of the one who needs it as I am stepping out in faith and ministering. We need to live like it is there at all times and conduct ourselves as if we have no limitations whatsoever…because we don't when it comes to fulfilling the purposes that God has for our lives. Notice that I did not say we have no financial limitations when buying a car or shopping for clothes! It is dangerous to try to apply spiritual truths when we are living according to the flesh.

"It is the spirit that quickeneth; the flesh profiteth nothing: the words that I speak unto you, they are spirit, and they are life" (John 6:63).

Having said all of these things we yet remain at the tip of the iceberg. The revelation and understanding that will come from comprehending higher dimensions will require many volumes. In the coming years, God will call Christians to operate on a much higher plane. A foundational understanding of our functionality among the higher dimensions, and within the second and third heavens will prove indispensable. On this note we are going to delve deeper into the trans-dimensional nature of the spirit and look at how it relates to activity in the second heaven.

CHAPTER 10

The Trans-Dimensional Nature of the Spirit

Let us return to our example of the line, the paper, and the room. In our example, we learned that the line represents one dimension, the paper represents two dimensions, and the room represents three dimensions. The next lesson we must take away from our example is that while higher dimensions contain equivalent and lower dimensions, lower dimensions cannot contain higher dimensions. Allow me to explain.

PREFACING THE TRANS-DIMENSIONAL DISCUSSION

I can draw a line on a piece of paper. When I do this, the paper contains the line. This is because the line only possesses one dimension, which is length. Since the paper possesses both length and width, I can put length onto the paper so that it is contained by the paper. I can also put a square shape on the paper. As long as its dimensions are smaller than that of the paper, the two-dimensional square can be contained by the two-dimensional paper. If the dimensions of the square happen to be larger than the dimensions of the paper, the two-dimensional square simply goes on to contain the two-dimensional paper. In any case, we realize that a particular dimension will contain lower dimensions along with structures having the same number of dimensions.

Conversely, I cannot fit a two-dimensional paper into a line that only contains length. This is impossible, because length does not permit width to manifest into its dimensional plane. Furthermore, while a three-dimensional room can contain a two-dimensional piece of paper, the two-dimensional paper cannot contain the three-dimensional room. The reason is because length and width do not permit height to manifest into their dimensional plane. Through the use of shading, angles, and other artistic techniques, it is possible to represent a three-dimensional object on a two dimensional-plane. However, it is impossible for the two-dimensional plane to actually *contain* a three-dimensional object.

Having established this premise, it follows that the same is true when traveling from the third dimension to the fourth dimension, and from the fifth dimension to the sixth dimension. This is where things gets interesting. Without a first dimension, you cannot have a second dimension. Furthermore, without a first dimension, you cannot have a third dimension. If I have a three-dimensional box and I try to eliminate the first dimension of length, all I am left with is height and width. This means that I have now reduced my total dimensions from three to two. *It is impossible to have a third-dimensional existence without occupying the first and second dimensions as well.*

A Glimpse of God's Nature

This leads us into understanding biblical language regarding the nature of God. While we will be discussing the omnipresence of God at depth in a later chapter, take note of the following verse for now. Notice that it speaks of Jesus as "filling all in all." This means that he exists both in and above the highest dimension, and therefore must exist across all lower dimensions as well. As referenced earlier, the Bible is clear that Jesus has ascended far above "all heavens" (Ephesians 4:10). This allows him to "fill all in all," since the reality of his existence fills every dimensional plane. The impact of him filling every dimensional plane results in every level of existence remaining in subjection to his authority. This is why he is "far above all principality and power," which are different types of angels and spirits (existing as dimensional beings) both good and bad. Furthermore, due to the fact that the Church is spoken of as his body, this becomes evidence that we are existing across all of these dimensions as well. Believers are the body of Christ, and we are also his fullness.

"[Jesus is] Far above all principality, and power, and might, and dominion, and every name that is named, not only in this world, but also in that which is to come: And hath put all things under his feet, and gave him to be the head over all things to **the church, Which is his body, the fulness of him that filleth all in all**" (Ephesians 1:21–23).

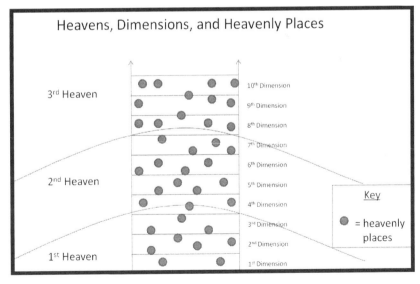

A GLIMPSE OF OUR NATURE

In the previous chapter, I explained that when we are saved by grace through faith in Jesus Christ, we are raised up and seated in heavenly places with him (Ephesians 2:6). Since these heavenly places are in him, it means that we are raised up into the third heaven in spirit. The illustration I have provided assumes that there are ten dimensions. This is in light of both the Superstring Theory and the desire to keep this discussion as simple as possible.

If there really are ten dimensions, and we are raised into the tenth dimension, then by simple logic we obtain additional evidence that <u>we also exist across all of the lower dimensions of the second heaven</u>. Since the beings and entities that occupy these dimensions of the second heaven (the fourth dimension, fifth dimension, sixth dimension, and so forth) would be able to perceive the activity of our spirits (existing across these dimensions), we get closer to understanding the meaning of the verse we referenced earlier. I have quoted the Amplified Bible this time to bring a fuller understanding of what is involved.

"[The purpose is] that through the church the complicated, many-sided wisdom of God in all its infinite variety and innumerable aspects might now be made known to the angelic rulers and authorities (principalities and powers) **in the heavenly sphere**. This is in accordance with the terms of the eternal and timeless purpose which He has realized and carried into effect in [the person of] Christ Jesus our Lord" (Ephesians 3:10–11 AMPC).

The Unredeemed

We have been focusing much of this study on the relevance it has to Christians. A question may have arisen by this point regarding the spirits of those who do not believe in Jesus Christ. On what dimension does the spirit of a non-Christian exist (or extend to)? I will answer this question by being completely frank. Pertaining to the state of the unredeemed human spirit, *I have no idea* which dimensional plane the spirit would cease to exist at. How can one answer the question: Does an unsaved person have a six-dimensional spirit or a seven-dimensional spirit? What I can state with considerable certainty is that since Jesus must "raise" us up to make us sit in his heavenly places, we must begin on a lower spiritual plane. Beyond this there is little else I have concluded with certainty. One intriguing possibility, according to an occult work known as the Emerald Tablets of Thoth, is that the unredeemed human spirit is four-dimensional, according to the following caption.

"Know ye, ye are threefold in nature, physical, astral and mental in one. Three are the qualities of each of the natures; nine in all, as above, so below... Three are the natures of the Astral, mediator is between above and below; not of the physical, not of the Spiritual, but able to move above and below... Above and beyond man's threefold nature lies the realm of **the Spiritual Self... <u>Four</u> is it in qualities, shining in each of the planes of existence**" (Secret of Secrets)[18]

As this is an occult work and also rather vague, I can't conclude with confidence that this answers the question. Even if I am properly relaying the information being communicated in this caption, who is to say it can be trusted? What I <u>can</u> say with complete conviction is that whatever dimension the unredeemed spirit extends to, it is perpetually vulnerable to the kingdom of darkness.

When I use the term *unredeemed spirit*, what I am referring to is the state of the spirit that does not have salvation in Jesus Christ. According to the Bible, being redeemed carries with it the idea of being ransomed. We are purchased with a price. We are purchased by God back into relationship and right standing with him through the sacrifice of Jesus Christ, who died on the cross for our sins. The Apostle Peter puts it this way.

"You must know (recognize) that you were **redeemed** (ransomed) from the useless (fruitless) way of living inherited by tradition from [your] forefathers, not with corruptible things [such as] silver and gold, But [you were purchased] with the precious blood of Christ (the Messiah), like that of a [sacrificial] lamb without blemish or spot" (1 Peter 1:18-19 AMPC).

In conclusion, while all human spirits have a trans-dimensional nature, those that have been redeemed by Jesus Christ exist at (or extend to) the highest dimension. However, due to our trans-dimensional nature, it actually leaves us susceptible to attacks and bondages that manifest from the dimensions of the second heaven. This is where the discussion of higher dimensions meets the discussion of spiritual warfare. The kingdom of light is at war with the kingdom of darkness. For this reason I am going to introduce the kingdom of darkness. This story begins with the fall of the cherub Lucifer.

CHAPTER 11

Introducing the Kingdom of Darkness

We will begin by setting up the typical misunderstanding of Satan and demonology. The theology most Christians believe goes something like this. Satan (also called Lucifer) is in heaven as the anointed cherub (Ezekiel 28:14). The multitude of his merchandise (Ezekiel 28:16) and the incredible beauty and wisdom he possesses (Ezekiel 28:17), among other things, leads to the iniquity that God finds in him (Ezekiel 28:15). As a result there is a war in heaven (Revelation 12:7–9) and God kicks Satan and his army of angels out (Revelation 12:4). This army comprises one-third of heaven's hosts. As a result of getting kicked out of heaven, Satan slams into earth. This is why Jesus says, "I saw Satan fall like lightening from heaven" (Luke 10:18). Satan is then present for the Garden of Eden incident, and all of the hosts of heaven that fall with him become demons. Is that simple enough?

The problem with this theology is that it's _too_ simple. Not only is it too simple, it's actually very sloppy when we begin to apply careful exegesis. In light of a proper understanding of the spirit realm, we will be able to glean a lot more information regarding the kingdom of darkness. This will leave us in a position of both preparedness and empowerment regarding the things that are coming on the earth.

INTRODUCING LUCIFER

In order to begin discussing the issue of fallen angels we will begin with Lucifer, the first and assumedly most powerful angel to rebel against God. The two famous passages dealing with the history of Lucifer are found in Ezekiel 28:12–19 and Isaiah 14:12–17. Interestingly enough, neither of these passages mention other angels joining him in his rebellion. While Lucifer did birth iniquity (Ezekiel 28:15), and as a result was cast out of the mountain of God as a profane thing (Ezekiel 28:16), it seems that at least *initially* he was relatively alone in these things. When Jesus mentions that he saw Satan fall from heaven like lightning, he does not mention any other angels falling with him. Furthermore, note that there was only one serpent in the Garden of Eden (Genesis 3). Not a serpent with a huge army.

"And He said to them, I saw Satan falling like a lightning [flash] from heaven" (Luke 10:18 AMPC).

UNDERSTANDING THE PRE-FLOOD WORLD

While this does not eliminate the possibility of angelic wars occurring before the creation of man, it certainly sets Satan apart when it comes to the angelic infiltration of earth. After the incident at the Garden of Eden, the Bible does not mention any more activity specifically attributed to Satan for a long time. However, the next event involving *heavenly hosts* occurs in Genesis 6. The story goes as follows:

"When people had spread all over the world, and daughters were being born, some of the **heavenly beings** saw that these young women were beautiful, so they took the ones they liked. Then the Lord said, I will not allow people to live forever; they are mortal. From now on they will live no longer than 120 years. In those days, and even later, **there were giants on the earth who were descendants of human women and the heavenly beings**. They were the great heroes and famous men of long ago" (Genesis 6:1–4 GNT).[19]

If you are a keen observer, you will note two things. One, this passage is incredibly clear on the fact that human women were impregnated by heavenly beings and gave birth to giants. Two, this is the Good News Translation (GNT) and not the King James Version. There is an obvious reason for this. In place of "heavenly beings," the KJV uses the term "sons of God," which some have attempted to argue away as the "sons of Seth" that sinfully intermingled with the "daughters of Cain." This exegetical foible is highly difficult to do with the GNT, which is why I use it here.

However, in order to dismantle any arguments, whether the English reads "heavenly beings" or "sons of God," the original Hebrew rendering is *b'nei Elohim*. This term is only used on three other occasions in the entire Bible, all in reference to angels (Job 1:6, 2:1, 38:7). To try and make the case that Genesis 6:1–4 is the only occasion that this terminology is not making reference to angels is a horrific violation of basic logic and biblical exegesis. Unfortunately, this is what quite a few individuals have tried to do. Therefore, to eliminate any confusion, it is easiest to use a translation that brings this point out in its English rendering, and the GNT does a fantastic job.

For those who theorize that Jesus said angels cannot have intercourse with women, all one has to do is reread what Jesus actually says in reference to this issue. He says that the "angels of God in heaven" don't marry. He says nothing of fallen angels marrying, and he certainly does not say that they are incapable of having intercourse with humans. All they would need is a physical body, and it doesn't seem like getting one is an obstacle for them. Frankly, how else could the Bible say that some have entertained angels unaware (Hebrews 13:2). If they always appeared in their spiritual form, *we would be aware!* This is what Jesus actually says:

"Jesus answered and said unto them, Ye do err, not knowing the Scriptures, nor the power of God. For in the resurrection they neither marry, nor are given in marriage, but are as the angels of God in heaven" (Matthew 22:29–30).

According to Genesis 6, giants began to exist because heavenly beings (or angels) began to produce offspring with human women. The fact that this has been a point of debate simply because people don't like the idea of angels impregnating women is admittedly upsetting. Nonetheless, there is a point to this discussion. The fact of the matter is that this was actually a separate rebellion from the fall of Lucifer. As a matter of fact, it was a rebellion based on different reasons. Lucifer rebelled *because* of the multitude of his merchandise, his beauty, and his corrupted wisdom (Ezekiel 28:16–17). The angels in Genesis 6 rebelled *because* they lusted after human women. This led to their harsh judgment.

"For if God **spared not the angels that sinned**, but cast them down to hell, and delivered them into chains of darkness, to be reserved unto judgment; And **spared not the old world**, but saved Noah the eighth person, a preacher of righteousness, bringing in the flood upon the world of the ungodly" (2 Peter 2:4–5).

The Bible is clear that the angels that sinned were cast down to hell and that God chose not to spare the old (pre-flood) world. These angels

118

that rebelled were locked up in chains under darkness until "the judgment of the great day." Since they were locked in hell while Satan wasn't, it actually suggests that Satan had little if anything to do with this rebellion.

"And the angels which kept not their **first estate**, but left their **own habitation**, he hath reserved in **everlasting chains under darkness** unto the judgment of the great day" (Jude 1:6).

According to the Book of Jude, these angels did not keep their first estate (Greek *arche*), which was their origin, or original heavenly appointment. They once had positions and assignments under God but abandoned them in order to execute this rebellion. Furthermore, they left their own habitations (Greek *oiketerion*). These were their spiritual bodies. In abandoning their "habitations," they assumed physical bodies in order to accommodate the act of physical union with human women. The fact that the term *oiketerion* is referring to their spiritual bodies is confirmed because the same term is used to describe the spiritual bodies we will one day receive.

"For we know that if our earthly house of this tabernacle were dissolved, we have a building of God, an house not made with hands, eternal in the heavens. For in this we groan, earnestly desiring to be clothed upon with our **house [*oiketerion*]** which is from heaven" (2 Corinthians 5:1–2).

THE WILD TRUTH REGARDING ANGELS

The idea that angels can put on physical bodies like humans put on clothes is illustrated when God and two angels visit Abraham. The background story is that God had come to inform Abraham that he would be having a son, even though both he and his wife were already old. God also informed him that he would be destroying Sodom and Gomorra. After leaving Abraham, the angels then proceeded to travel to Sodom and Gomorra where they met Lot to deliver him. That these angels were wearing physical bodies is obvious because they ate food and had their feet washed.

"And the LORD appeared unto him in the plains of Mamre: and he sat in the tent door in the heat of the day; And he lift up his eyes and looked, and, lo, three men [the LORD and two angels] stood by him: and when he saw them, he ran to meet them from the tent door, and bowed himself toward the ground, And said, My LORD, if now I have found favour in thy sight, pass not away, I pray thee, from thy servant: Let a little water, I pray you, be fetched, and **wash your feet**, and rest yourselves under the tree… And he took butter, and milk, and the calf which he had dressed, and set it before them; and he stood by them under the tree, and **they did eat**" (Genesis 18:1–4, 8).

Thus, it is established that physical union between an angel and a human woman is not really much of a feat at all. The rebelling angels assumed physical bodies and began to have children with the human women. These children were hybrids, being half-human and half-angelic, and as a result of their hybrid nature they were also giants when compared with normal men. This is why the Bible says, "In those days, and even later, there were giants on the earth who were descendants of human women and the heavenly beings" (Genesis 6:4 GNT).[20]

AN IMPORTANT ANCIENT TEXT

There exists an important ancient text known as *The Book of Enoch* or *1 Enoch*. Although it is not canonized, it is quoted by the Bible and provides information that the Bible is relatively silent on. Note how it is quoted by the Bible:

"And Enoch also, the seventh from Adam, prophesied of these, saying, Behold, the Lord cometh with ten thousands of his saints, To execute judgment upon all, and to convince all that are ungodly among them of all their ungodly deeds which they have ungodly committed, and of all their hard speeches which ungodly sinners have spoken against him" (Jude 1:14-15).

"And behold! He cometh with ten thousands of His holy ones, To execute judgment upon all, and to destroy all the ungodly: And to convict all flesh Of all the works of their ungodliness which they have ungodly committed, And of all the hard things which ungodly sinners have spoken against Him" (1 Enoch 1:9).[21]

The following quote is from the Book of 1 Enoch and, if it is correct, sheds additional light on the incident of Genesis 6:1–4. It helps us to understand that there were exactly 200 angels involved in the incident. Furthermore, the record in 1 Enoch confirms a non-traditional idea. Lucifer had little if anything to do with this rebellion.[22] His name is not listed among the names of the captains.

"And it came to pass when the children of men had multiplied that in those days were born unto them beautiful and comely daughters. And the angels, the children of the heaven, saw and lusted after them, and said to one another: 'Come, let us choose us wives from among the children of men and beget us children...' Then sware they all together and bound themselves by mutual imprecations upon it. And they were in all **two hundred**; who descended in the days of Jared on the summit of Mount Hermon, and they called it Mount Hermon, because they had sworn and bound themselves by mutual imprecations upon it. And these are the names of their leaders: Samlazaz, their leader, Araklba, Rameel, Kokablel, Tamlel, Ramlel, Danel, Ezeqeel, Baraqijal, Asael, Armaros, Batarel, Ananel, Zaqlel, Samsapeel, Satarel, Turel, Jomjael, Sariel. These are their chiefs of tens" (1 Enoch 6:1–3a, 5b–8).[23]

THE WILD TRUTH REGARDING GIANTS

Thus far, everything we have discussed has been in relation to angels. However, now that we have established what Genesis 6 actually explains, we can move on. The word translated as *giants* in the Book of Genesis is the Hebrew word *nephilim*. It was primarily due to *nephilim* activity that the flood was sent. This activity threatened a pure human seed, which would be necessary to bring about the birth of the Messiah. In other words, without direct intervention, the proliferation of these hybrids may have led to the extinction of a pure human seed. God could not let that happen. Moreover, this activity also played a role in bringing about total lawlessness and evil (Genesis 6:5). Thus, God sent the flood.

After the flood, the *nephilim* showed up again, particularly in the Promised Land (Canaan). When they showed up they were divided into different races. Some of them are listed below:

> ➤ Rephaims: a tall ancient people in the land east of the Jordan. The dead ones (Genesis 14:5)

> ➤ Emims: Fearful ones (Deuteronomy 2:11–12)

> ➤ Anakims: long-necked ones (Deuteronomy 2:11–12)

> ➤ Zamzummims: (Deuteronomy 2:20)

> ➤ Horims: a race of nephilim conquered by the descendants of Esau (Deuteronomy 2:12)

> Avims: Conquered by the Caphtorims (Deuteronomy 2:23)

> Caphtorims: giants from the lineage of Mizraim (Egypt) (1 Chronicles 1:11–12)

THE WILD TRUTH ABOUT DEMONS

Etymologically related to the Hebrew word *Rephaim* (one of the tribes of the giants) is the Hebrew word *rapha*. They both carry the connotation of being dead—*rapha* referring to the dead *Rephaim*. It is no coincidence that *rapha* actually means "ghost" or "shade" according to Strong's Concordance. This leads us to a particularly interesting passage in the Book of Isaiah. In this passage, the prophet is prophesying about the resurrection of the dead; more specifically, how we should rejoice about the coming fulfillment of this promise.

"Your dead shall live [O Lord]; the bodies of our dead [saints] shall rise. You who dwell in the dust, awake and sing for joy! For Your dew [O Lord] is a dew of [sparkling] light [heavenly, supernatural dew]; and the earth shall cast forth the dead [to life again; for on the land of the shades of the dead You will let Your dew fall]" (Isaiah 26:19 AMPC).

From the Book of Revelation we learn that there are two resurrections. One resurrection is for those who have died in Christ (Revelation 20:5–6), and the other is for everyone else (Revelation 20:12–13). The important point is that every human will experience a resurrection for judgment at some point. It is impossible to be human and not receive a resurrection, unless we happen to be part of the population of Christians that "are alive and remain" at his second coming and get "changed" (1 Corinthians 15:51-52, 1 Thessalonians 4:15–17). Isaiah 26 is very important because, while the Book of Revelation is clear that all humans will receive a resurrection, Isaiah seems to suggest that some won't. How is this possible?

"They are dead, they shall not live; they are **deceased, <u>they shall not rise</u>**: therefore hast thou visited and destroyed them, and made all their memory to perish" (Isaiah 26:14 NKJV).

How are there some "deceased" that will not rise? The word *deceased* has been bolded because it is translated from the Hebrew word *rapha*. Remember that while this word means "ghost" or "shade," it is etymologically related to the word *Rephaim*. In essence, Isaiah is actually saying that as ghosts, the spirits of dead nephilim will not have a resurrection from God. You may be thinking that this seems like a slight stretch, but trying to interpret it as pertaining to humans is straightforwardly impossible. This is the only conclusion that makes sense. As we read this verse in the Amplified Bible, it only continues to verify this point. Notice the use of the word *ghost*.

"They [the former tyrant masters] are dead, they shall not live *and* reappear; they are powerless **ghosts**, they shall not rise *and* come back. Therefore You have visited and made an end of them and caused every memory of them [every trace of their supremacy] to perish" (Isaiah 26:14 AMPC).

Although Isaiah doesn't go on to specifically tell us what comes of these departed spirits, the fact that the word *rapha* means "ghosts" or "shades" is enough to draw our conclusion. Demons are not angels, but the disembodied spirits of dead nephilim. Having proven this with the Bible, we can verify it by returning to the account of 1 Enoch.

And now, the giants, who are produced from the spirits and flesh, shall be called evil spirits upon the earth, and on the earth shall be their dwelling. Evil spirits have proceeded from their bodies; because they are born from men and from the holy Watchers is their beginning and primal origin; they shall be evil spirits on earth, and evil spirits shall they be called. [As for the spirits of heaven, in heaven shall be their dwelling, but as for the spirits of the earth which were born upon the earth, on the earth shall be their dwelling.] And the spirits of the giants afflict, oppress, destroy, attack, do battle, and work destruction on the earth, and cause trouble: they take no food, but nevertheless hunger and thirst, and cause offences. And these spirits shall rise up against the children of men and against the women, because they have proceeded from them.

(1 Enoch 15:8–12)[24]

CHAPTER 12

Victory over the Darkness

Angels and demons are, in fact, entities of two different classes. While angels are the direct creation of God, demons are the disembodied spirits of dead hybrids. We are now going to continue our discussion on the topic of angels. We have already gone over the fact that Lucifer was the first angel to rebel. However, as we took a closer look at what happened during the Genesis 6 incident, we realized that Lucifer had little if any involvement in that rebellion. This is further proven in that while the angels discussed in Genesis 6 were cast into hell (2 Peter 2:4–5) and placed in everlasting chains under darkness (Jude 1:6), Satan wasn't. Satan was clearly roaming the earth during the time of Job.

"Now there was a day when the sons of God came to present themselves before the LORD, and **Satan came also among them**. And the LORD said unto Satan, Whence comest thou? Then Satan answered the LORD, and said, **From going to and fro in the earth**, and from walking up and down in it" (Job 1:6–7).

The fact that there were two separate rebellions proves something vitally important for us to understand. There were, and have historically been, <u>multiple angelic rebellions</u>. This leads us into the twelfth chapter of the Book of Revelation. Instead of jumping right into a particular verse and using it out of context to prove something we think we should believe, we will start at the beginning.

A Great Wonder

"And there appeared a great wonder in heaven; a woman clothed with the sun, and the moon under her feet, and upon her head a crown of twelve stars: And she being with child cried, travailing in birth, and pained to be delivered" (Revelation 12:1–2).

The passage begins by describing a great wonder in heaven. As we proceed to define this wonder, we are going to allow the Bible to interpret itself. In other words, where do we see the Bible using the same imagery, and how does that fit with what we are being presented here? In the Book of Genesis, one of the twelve sons of Jacob is Joseph. Jacob was the son of Isaac and the grandson of Abraham. He was later renamed Israel by God. His son Joseph had a dream in which the sun, the moon and eleven stars bowed down to him. That dream was interpreted by Jacob, who responded as follows:

"And he told it to his father, and to his brethren: and his father rebuked him, and said unto him, What is this dream that thou hast dreamed? **Shall I and thy mother and thy brethren indeed come to bow down ourselves to thee to the earth?**" (Genesis 37:10).

Based on this interpretation, Jacob is represented by the sun, his wife is represented by the moon, and the twelve stars are the twelve tribes of Israel (Joseph being the twelfth star). Thus, the woman who is in the midst of all of these symbols represents the nation of Israel. It should come as no surprise that Israel is represented by a woman on numerous occasions throughout Scripture (Hosea 3:1, Ezekiel 36:17). Therefore, Revelation 12:2 is most likely describing the time when the nation of Israel was ready to deliver the Messiah to the world.[25] In my opinion, this is the most accurate exegetical timeframe for the next comment.

THE DRAGON AND THE CHILD

"And there appeared another wonder in heaven; and behold a great red dragon, having seven heads and ten horns, and seven crowns upon his heads. And his tail drew the third part of the stars of heaven, and did cast them to the earth: and the dragon stood before the woman which was ready to be delivered, for to devour her child as soon as it was born" (Revelation 12:3–4).

As we read the next portion of Scripture, we see a dragon having seven heads and ten horns. We know that this is a symbolic representation of Satan because Revelation 12:9 says so. Regarding the seven heads and ten horns: heads on a beast are scripturally significant of successive kingdoms, while horns tend to mean rulers within a kingdom. The passage goes on to explain that the tail of this dragon draws a third of the stars of heaven and casts them to the earth. Allowing the Bible to define itself in the most logical manner, stars in this case are symbolic of angelic beings (Revelation 1:20).

According to longstanding tradition, which has been forgotten by much of the Church, there are nine choirs of heavenly hosts. These "stars" are most likely comprised of angelic beings from all nine of these choirs. These nine choirs of angels are easily extracted from the canon biblical texts. This revelation is also confirmed by an occult text known as the Sixth Book of Moses.[26] I only reference this work to point out that occult practitioners are well aware of the nine choirs of heavenly beings, while many Christians remain uninformed. The nine choirs of heavenly beings (with Scripture references) are as follows:

1. Seraphim (Isaiah 6:2)
2. Cherubim (Genesis 3:24)
3. Thrones (Colossians 1:16)
4. Dominions (Colossians 1:16)
5. Virtues [also known as Mights] (Ephesians 1:21)
6. Powers (Ephesians 6:12)
7. Principalities (Ephesians 6:12)
8. Archangels (Jude 1:9)
9. Angels (Psalm 103:20)

I will mention that some may add to this list the *Ophanim*, which are the "wheels" that are present in Ezekiel's vision (Ezekiel 1:16). Transitioning back to Revelation 12, notice that in verse 4, the purpose for drawing them to the earth is clearly given. It is to devour the child, the Messiah, as soon as he is born. Furthermore, the timeframe for this angelic rebellion led by Lucifer does not seem to be prior to the Garden of Eden (when taken in context). While I am not so bold as to say that it is impossible that this verse could be referring to an event prior to the Garden of Eden, I want to suggest that there may be an equally possible alternative.

If we accurately exegete the passage and simply read what it says, it gives us a timeframe of some point prior to the birth of Jesus (but after Israel becomes a nation). The problem with interpreting this event as occurring prior to the creation of earth and man is summed up in the following way. The first prophecy of the Messiah doesn't occur until God judges Adam, Eve, and the Serpent (Genesis 3:15). How could Satan lead one-third of the "stars of heaven" in rebellion *to devour the Messiah* prior to the first revelation of God's plan to send a Messiah (Jesus Christ)? Revelation 12:4 is very clear that the *express purpose* for the rebellion was to devour the Messiah as soon as he was born.

Verses 5 and 6 go on to discuss that Jesus was born anyway, he was not devoured, and he was ultimately caught up unto God. Jesus lived, died a horrific death upon the cross, and was raised to life. He was caught up into heaven not too long afterwards. Verse 6 goes on to discuss the "woman" and how she will flee into a place prepared for her in the wilderness for 1,260 days. The most popular approach to this passage suggests that this correlates with the timeframe given for the coming great tribulation, meaning that this text could be jumping forward in time (Daniel 9:27, Daniel 11:31, Matthew 24:15–21, Revelation 13:5–7). I am not entirely convinced that this is the best application of this particular verse in context, but at present, I do not have a better interpretation to offer. Regardless of what we do with verse 6, verse 7 is established as a separate thought.

A GREAT WAR

"And there was war in heaven: Michael and his angels fought against the dragon; and the dragon fought and his angels, And prevailed not; neither was their place found any more in heaven. And the great dragon was cast out, that old serpent, called the Devil, and Satan, which deceiveth the whole world: he was cast out into the earth, and his angels were cast out with him" (Revelation 12:7–9).

We are now at a significant war in heaven. In this war, Satan and the fallen angels with him are cast out of heaven (specifically the third heaven). This comes after a battle with the archangel Michael and his angels. The question is: when does this war take place? Some have suggested that it happened prior to the Garden of Eden. This group includes many of those who believe that when Satan *initially* rebelled, he led one-third of the angels in rebellion with him. My question is: If this were true, why was

Satan still coming before God in the Book of Job? The problem with this interpretation is that the passage is clear—after this war, *their place was no longer* found *in heaven*. If this war took place before the Garden of Eden, Satan would not have retained the authority necessary to access the third heaven for his appearance in the Book of Job (and again in Zechariah 3:1). This doesn't mean Satan or his minions can't be brought before the throne of God, but they certainly don't retain the authority to come and go as they please. This privilege has been allocated to the children of God (Hebrews 4:16).

Others have said that this war is yet to come. They suggest that during the great tribulation, Satan will make war with heaven. The great tribulation is defined as a three-and-a-half-year period at the end of the age (Matthew 24:21). During this time, a biblical character known most popularly by the title "antichrist" (1 John 2:18) will do a majority of his damage. Could Revelation 12:7–9 be referring to a war in heaven during this timeframe? I don't believe so, particularly because this interpretation gives little explanation for the results of the war (which we will discuss shortly).

I am firmly persuaded that this war *actually* occurred and came to its end during the time that Jesus conducted his ministry on earth. This may seem like an odd approach, but I believe it is the most logical interpretation. Having said all of this, there is a question that still warrants discussion. What are we to do with the revelation that Jesus was the Lamb slain from the foundation of the world (Revelation 13:8)? In other words, if Jesus was slain from the foundation of the world, what if this war was also fought from the foundation of the world? This would take us back to the first common conclusion, which is that this war is pre-Adamic.

My response is that although Jesus was slain from the foundation of the world, this fact was a mystery hidden in the mind of God. This is why Satan cooperated in the murder of Jesus. If he knew the plan of God, or that Jesus was slain from the foundation of the world, he would not have cooperated. I believe that this war may have played out in the mind of

God long before it manifested relative to our timeline. If this is true, then it would also have been hidden from understanding, just like the death, burial, and resurrection of Jesus Christ. At some point it had to manifest into our timeline, and I believe the time of its manifestation aligns with the finished work of Jesus Christ. This leads us into the very next verse: Revelation 12:10.

Now is Come...

"And there was war in heaven: Michael and his angels fought against the dragon; and the dragon fought and his angels, And prevailed not; neither was their place found any more in heaven. And the great dragon was cast out, that old serpent, called the Devil, and Satan, which deceiveth the whole world: he was cast out into the earth, and his angels were cast out with him. And I heard a loud voice saying in heaven, **Now is come [1] salvation, and [2] strength, and the [3] kingdom of our God, and the [4] power of his Christ**: for the accuser of our brethren is cast down, which accused them before our God day and night" (Revelation 12:7–10).

Verse 10 is the true crux of this passage. It describes the results of the war, and *when we understand the results, we realize that these are the promises associated with the salvation we currently possess.* These promises didn't come prior to the Garden of Eden, nor are we still waiting for them. In other words, because of the stated results, this war <u>must</u> have ended prior to the resurrection of Jesus. As we will discover, the true ending of this war came as a result of the work that Jesus accomplished between his death and resurrection. Let's begin by looking at the results.

1. <u>Salvation</u> - "That if thou shalt confess with thy mouth the Lord Jesus, and shalt believe in thine heart that God hath raised him from the dead, thou shalt be saved. For with the

heart man believeth unto righteousness; and with the mouth confession is made unto **salvation**" (Romans 10:9–10).

2. <u>Strength</u> – "And he said unto me, My grace is sufficient for thee: for my **strength** is made perfect in weakness. Most gladly therefore will I rather glory in my infirmities, that the power of Christ may rest upon me" (2 Corinthians 12:9). "I can do all things through Christ which **strengtheneth** me" (Philippians 4:13).

3. <u>Kingdom</u> - "I John, who also am your brother, and companion in tribulation, and in the **kingdom** and patience of Jesus Christ, was in the isle that is called Patmos, for the word of God, and for the testimony of Jesus Christ" (Revelation 1:9). "Who hath delivered us from the power of darkness, and hath translated us into the **kingdom** of his dear Son" (Colossians 1:13).

4. <u>Power of his Christ</u> - "And he said unto me, My grace is sufficient for thee: for my strength is made perfect in weakness. Most gladly therefore will I rather glory in my infirmities, that the **power of Christ** may rest upon me" (2 Corinthians 12:9).

"Verily, verily, I say unto you, he that believeth on me, the works that I do shall he do also; and **greater works** than these shall he do; because I go unto my Father. And whatsoever ye shall ask in my name, that will I do, that the Father may be glorified in the Son" (John 14:12–13).

Could the Bible really be any clearer about what resulted from this war? I don't think so. Everything that came about with the end of this war aligns perfectly with what the Bible discusses relative to the promises of salvation in Jesus Christ. Therefore, this becomes the third definite angelic rebellion, the first being the fall of Lucifer, and the second being the rebellion of the angels involved in Genesis 6. Moving forward, it can be concluded that it was the hosts of heaven referenced by Revelation 12:4 that Jesus spoiled and triumphed over between his death and resurrection.

"And having spoiled **principalities** and **powers** [types of angelic spirits], he made a shew of them openly, triumphing over them in it" (Colossians 2:15).

This is why, when Jesus was resurrected, he explained that he had all authority in heaven and on earth (Matthew 28:18). This is also why we now have the victory in all things through Christ Jesus (1 Corinthians 15:57). However, this is not where the story ends. By the time we reach the New Testament Epistles, we are told where the rebellious heavenly hosts (not associated with the pre-flood incident) are currently found. We are told that they reside in heavenly places. Which heavenly places? These would be heavenly places of the second heaven. The question is, how did they end up there; and furthermore, what does this mean for us?

"For we are not wrestling with flesh and blood [contending only with physical opponents], but against the despotisms, against the powers, against [the master spirits who are] the world rulers of this present darkness, against the spirit forces of wickedness in the heavenly (supernatural) sphere" (Ephesians 6:12 AMPC).

CHAPTER 13

The Coming Darkness

The fallen angels that rebelled with Lucifer in Revelation 12:4 are largely found in the heavenly places of the second heaven. This is where spiritual warfare must be conducted across multiple dimensional planes. While there do seem to be some fallen angels that roam the earth—like Satan (1 Peter 5:8)—many of them seem to be trapped or kept where they are. Remember that when they were cast down after the war of Revelation 12:7, they were not cast to the earth, but just cast out of the realm of the third heaven. They were cast out into the heavenly places of the second heaven. The only heavenly being specifically cast to the earth as a result of this war (according to Scripture) was Satan himself. Satan was cast to the earth. Satan's angels were simply cast out.

"And the great dragon was cast out, that old serpent, called the Devil, and Satan, which deceiveth the whole world: **he was cast out into the earth**, and his **angels were cast out** with him" (Revelation 12:9).

This is why certain occult groups will conduct very powerful rituals to bring these beings over for brief amounts of time in order to communicate with them. They are trapped in the heavens and must be accessed and brought in by the efforts and rituals of people. One individual who turned from extreme darkness to Jesus Christ described to me, in great detail, what happens during these rituals. His name is Robert Vandriest Mitchell, and he defected from the Illuminati. I was told that a certain combination of time (ideally between 2:00 a.m. and 4:00 a.m.), locations (such as ley lines), along with significant astrological alignments, can allow for portals to be opened with powerful rituals. Ley lines are believed to be the spiritual alignment of land forms and sacred or ancient sites.

Under the right conditions, a powerful ritual performed with an incantation incorporating certain tonal projections, often paired with blood sacrifices, will open a ball of light in midair. It opens up in a sort of soundless explosion, *and this ball of light is the portal.* It is not a circle, but a sphere. Out of this portal various types of physical and non-physical entities can come in for a temporary period of time. Humans can use these portals to cross over to other realms as well. In support of this report, consider this testimony from one woman who claims to have been involved with this kind of activity.

ENGAGING DARK POWERS

...during the rituals, you had to have psychic ability. You have to be very powerful in that way to call out The Old Ones...that come from another dimension. They actually materialize from out of another dimension, and are present at rituals. And they are so powerful, and there is such an evilness about them, that they want out of this other dimension. And they have to be called out by someone who has that power.

—Arizona Wilder[27]

Not only can they be brought here, but there are apparently ways for humans to travel to where these beings are located. Consider this quote:

Archiometry… is a very advanced branch of black magic and voodoo, which involves cultivating the ability to enter into alternate universes, and then you go into these universes and you try and energize the universe, become the god of that universe, and then draw power from that universe back into your own universe. This started out, basically, as part of the worship of the star god Sirius, which is known in Egypt as Set, which is the Egyptian version of the Devil. The idea is that because there was a black dwarf star of Sirius next to the white star Sirius, it became known as Sirius A and Sirius B. Ancient magicians realized that they could use that black star as a gateway into an alternate universe, and so that's how they discovered universe B. Then later on there was universe C and D and E and etcetera, etcetera… The person who comes back invariably seems to have amped up their power by a whole order of magnitude… It's believed by these people [that] this is a very easy way of becoming a living god… The fact of the matter is [that] you're doing it by demonic power and if you're indeed entering other universes those are universes that are populated by extremely evil beings and extremely wise cruel beings.

—Bill Schnoebelen[28]

Another woman named Carolyn Hamlett testifies to a large number of experiences involving fallen angels, the Luciferian hierarchy, and activity occurring in other dimensions. She testifies that one of her jobs before getting saved and delivered by Jesus Christ was to go to other dimensions and bring in what she described as light beings. She describes these entities as the "big brass"—entities that were being brought in for the final phases of "the plan."[29] "The plan" is a reference to the final stand of the kingdom of darkness in its efforts to confront the Lord Jesus at his coming and to deceive humanity.

THE RESTRAINER

What keeps these beings where they are? I propose that this is the job of the restrainer referenced in 2 Thessalonians 2:7. This is the force that is primarily responsible for maintaining the divide or "veil" that separates our dimension from the dimensions where many of these fallen angels are trapped.

"Do you not recollect that when I was still with you, I told you these things? And now you know what is restraining him [from being revealed at this time]; it is so that he may be manifested (revealed) in his own [appointed] time. For the mystery of lawlessness (that hidden principle of rebellion against constituted authority) is already at work in the world, [but it is] restrained only until **he who restrains** is taken out of the way" (2 Thessalonians 2:5–7 AMPC).

In order to understand the job of "he who restrains," it really becomes necessary to understand what the mystery of lawlessness is. The word translated as *mystery* is the Greek word *musterion*. This word primarily means "truth revealed." In the Roman culture this was understood as the information known to the *mustes*, or initiated ones.[30] The initiated ones were the practitioners of the mystery religions. In other words, the mysteries were the secret knowledge practiced and passed down by occult adepts. Here Paul makes the distinction "mystery of lawlessness" because he uses the same word (*musterion*) in other writings to refer to mysteries found in

Christ. Here he wants us to know that the activity associated with mystery religions was well and alive in the earth. This is still true today.

Mystery religions practice the occult. That's what they do. They are responsible for doing rituals associated with summoning demons, or even fallen angels. In order to summon certain fallen angels, they must be called out of their dimensions and into ours. This means that the mysteries these people practice will allow them to sidestep, so-to-speak, the barrier that separates our dimension from others. It is this activity that Paul is relating to the work of the restrainer. In other words, while the restrainer maintains dimensional separation, there is an ongoing effort to sidestep what the restrainer was put there to do.

I'm not going to try to prove the identity of the restrainer to you but I will say this: the text does not tell us who it is. Some say it's the Holy Spirit. This may be true. In my opinion, the restrainer is most likely some sort of super-powerful angelic being. Whoever the restrainer is, the singular personal pronoun "he" seems to indicate that this is some type of entity.

In any case, he will one day be taken out of the way. If you have followed me up to this point, then you have probably figured out what I am getting at. The problem is that when the force is removed that separates the earth from the dimensions where many fallen angels are trapped, our world will quickly change in many ways that elude the imagination. Today we deal with disembodied spirits of dead nephilim. These are the demons. They are like cupcakes when compared with the power of beings that are the direct creation of God.

Consider this: the angel of the Lord killed 185,000 men in one night (2 Kings 19:35). No destruction like this has ever been affiliated with a petty demon. We are talking about two entirely different classes of entities. Are we really prepared for spiritual warfare to move to a whole other echelon? In Christ we have the victory, but we need to be prepared to enforce it. As what I am explaining to you begins to manifest, those who are unprepared and those who are lukewarm will undoubtedly fall away.

THE MANIFESTATION OF THE LAWLESS ONE

The passage in 2 Thessalonians 2 continues to link the removal of the restrainer to the manifestation of the lawless one, otherwise known as the antichrist.

"And then the lawless one (the antichrist) will be revealed and the Lord Jesus will slay him with the breath of His mouth and bring him to an end by His appearing at His coming. The coming [of the lawless one, the antichrist] is through the activity and working of Satan and will be attended by great power and with all sorts of [pretended] miracles and signs and delusive marvels--[all of them] lying wonders--And by unlimited seduction to evil and with all wicked deception for those who are perishing (going to perdition) because they did not welcome the Truth but refused to love it that they might be saved" (2 Thessalonians 2:8–10 AMPC).

Notice that as we learn about the coming of the antichrist, the Bible is clear that many signs, pretend miracles, and lying wonders will accompany him. I am convinced that this aligns with what the Bible says regarding the sixth seal. Sure enough, as we read about the sixth seal in the Book of Revelation, we find that "stars will fall to the earth." These will include the stars (angels) that are currently kept from us by the restrainer—they will return.

"And I beheld when he had opened the sixth seal, and, lo, there was a great earthquake; and the sun became black as sackcloth of hair, and the moon became as blood; And **the stars of heaven fell unto the earth**, even as a fig tree casteth her untimely figs, when she is shaken of a mighty wind" (Revelation 6:12-13).[31]

Now that we have established that many fallen angels will be coming to the earth at some point in the future, we have greater clarity on what Jesus meant when he said that the last days would be like the days of Noah. Noah lived prior to the great flood. There was a point prior to the great flood when fallen angels, their children, other related abominations, and men all occupied the earth at once. As it was in the days of Noah, so shall it be in the days of the coming of the Son of Man.

"And as it was in the **days** of [**Noah**], so shall it be also in the **days** of the Son of man" (Luke 17:26).

MORE ON HYBRIDS

However, even in saying all of this, there is still activity I have yet to address. We have established a scriptural understanding for many things, but now we are prepared to dive even deeper. What of genetic engineering and the creation of hybrid creatures and abominations? Does the Bible speak of hybrid creatures? Did things like centaurs and nagas exist? Could they exist today? Let's begin our conversation around the satyr. A satyr, according to mythology, was a human/goat hybrid. Does the Bible acknowledge their existence? Absolutely!

"But wild beasts of the desert shall lie there; and their houses shall be full of doleful creatures; and owls shall dwell there, and **satyrs** shall dance there" (Isaiah 13:21).

The most common rebuttal I get when I point this verse out to skeptics is that their version of the Bible translates this word as shaggy goat. Could it be that the translators of the King James Version were just being sloppy?

"But desert creatures will lie down there, And their houses will be full of owls; Ostriches also will live there, and **shaggy goats** will frolic there" (Isaiah 13:21 NASB).[32]

Let's take a closer look, shall we? The Hebrew word translated *satyr* in Isaiah 13:21 is the word *sa'iyr*. According to the definition given by Strong's Concordance, this word can mean a "devil," "a goat," "a kid," "hairy," "rough," or "satyr." So how do we distinguish what meaning is actually being implied here? To answer this question, we will look at two seemingly unrelated Scriptures.

"And they shall no more offer their sacrifices unto **devils**, after whom they have gone a whoring. This shall be a statute for ever unto them throughout their generations" (Leviticus 17:7).

"And he [Rehoboam, son of Solomon] ordained him priests for the high places, and for the **devils**, and for the calves which he had made" (2 Chronicles 11:15).

So what do these verses have to do with our topic? Everything! Notice that the word *devils* is bolded in both passages. The Hebrew word translated *devils* in these passages is—you guessed it—*sa'yir*! God literally rebuked the Israelites for making sacrifices to satyrs after he delivered them from Egypt. The Israelites actually *whored* themselves after these creatures. Moreover, Rehoboam moved to reinstitute this type of sacrifice and worship. The hybrids were real because the Bible says so—plain and simple.

Moreover, we must understand that the Bible reveals to us that these hybrids were inherently evil. It straightforwardly associates these creatures with a demonic nature in the original language and word use. This is our biblical premise for moving further into this study. The Bible supports the concept of hybrids, and it helps us to understand that when they occur, their nature is demonic. It can be deduced by simple logic that, like *nephilim*, when hybrid creatures die, their spirits also join the spirit realm as demons. They are not treated like human spirits, and they are certainly not angels.

It is true that the Bible does not make reference to every creature referenced by various mythologies. However, by simply understanding that the Bible speaks about the existence of hybrids, it makes room for the possibility that any and all of the so-called mythological creatures of other cultures may have existed at one time. This leaves us at a veritable Pandora's Box. How do hybrid creatures come about, and what is the agenda behind their creation?

In the Book of Revelation, we find that during the fifth trumpet judgment, bizarre creatures are being loosed from a place called the pit. The pit actually resides in another dimension. It's not something you will encounter while driving to your local grocery store. The king over this place is a fallen angel named Abaddon. It is from this passage that we can begin to gain a better understanding regarding hybrid creatures.

> And the fifth angel sounded, and I saw a star fall from heaven unto the earth: and to him was given the key of the bottomless pit. And he opened the bottomless pit; and there arose a smoke out of the pit, as the smoke of a great furnace; and the sun and the air were darkened by reason of the smoke of the pit. And there came out of the smoke locusts upon the earth: and unto them was given power, as the scorpions of the earth have power...And the shapes of the locusts were like unto horses prepared unto battle; and on their heads were as it were crowns like gold, and their faces were as the faces of men. And they had hair as the hair of women, and their teeth were as the teeth of lions. And they had breastplates, as it were breastplates of iron; and the sound of their wings was as the

sound of chariots of many horses running to battle. And they had tails like unto scorpions, and there were stings in their tails: and their power was to hurt men five months. And they had a king over them, which is the angel of the bottomless pit, whose name in the Hebrew tongue is Abaddon, but in the Greek tongue hath his name Apollyon.

(Revelation 9:1–3, 7–11)

When we go into the original language, it is confirmed that the entire description of these creatures is anatomical. Even the breastplates that this passage describes are an anatomical feature of these abominations. They are very much physical in nature and they are described as part human, part horse, part scorpion, and part lion, with something else mixed in there to cause them to grow wings. What do you call a living organism that appears like this? It is a hybrid. When we take into account that their king is a fallen angel, we also glean that the agenda to create hybrid creatures is something that originates with fallen angels. This allows fallen angels to expand the army of darkness. When hybrid creatures die, their spirits are then subjugated, and still used to further the satanic agenda.

Although these particular hybrids of Revelation 9 are specifically reserved for release at the fifth trumpet, the agenda for hybrids has never been limited to the last days. Hybrids clearly existed in the Old Testament, and with thousands of years to refine their technologies, what do you think Satan and his minions are up to today? They are tinkering with all kinds of possibilities in order to create their own army. Why don't we see them today? I personally believe that much of the work being done to this end has taken place in the heavenly places (or other dimensions) where fallen angels are located. As we have just established, hybrids will be released from the pit, which exists in another dimension. Some things do seem to take place on earth, usually as part of black projects in underground bases, but

146

hard evidence on this claim is virtually impossible to produce. Therefore, I will simply leave you to do your own research in respect to this issue.

I want to make it very clear that today angels are not alone in working on this kind of thing, but humans are involved as well. A news article was released reporting that 150 human-animal hybrid embryos were grown in UK labs.[33] As a matter of fact, one woman who goes by the pseudonym "Axe" actually testifies to being used as a "psychic" in order to astrally project into the bodies of hybrid creatures that could not talk (being grown in underground bases as part of black projects) to assess their thoughts and feelings.

The conclusion of the matter is that all of these problems are our responsibility as God's people in the earth. We will be confronted with all of these forms of evil, and we will be called to continue to establish the victory of Jesus Christ in spite of them. The only reason any of this would scare a Christian is if that person's view of God were too small. If you're scared, it's time to change your perspective on just how powerful God is. Not only does God have solutions to all of these problems, he has chosen *you* to be a part of the army that he will use to confront them. Even if you don't want to, it is my assessment that the day will come when you won't have a choice.

However, in order to confront these things by utilizing the resources that God has made available to us, we must resolve identity issues. In other words, we must embrace the identity that he has given us. This is a prerequisite to manifesting his kingdom through our lives. In order to do this, it requires that we not only understand our identity in Christ, but also what our identity entitles us to. This leads us into our next discussion. The Bible is clear that God is sovereign, all-powerful, all-knowing, everywhere present, and the Creator of heaven and earth. It then goes on to say that we have been made partakers of the divine nature (2 Peter 1:4). What does this mean in light of all that we have discussed thus far? The answer will forever transform you.

CHAPTER 14

Sharing in the Divine Nature

Knowing God intimately is something that every Christian should experience. God wants to have a flourishing love relationship with you and me. He wants a relationship that goes so deep, its passion transcends time and space (literally). Knowing God in this way is an essential attribute of those whom the Lord will use to execute great exploits in the last days. In the Book of Daniel, the angel informs the prophet as follows:

"And such as do wickedly against the covenant shall he corrupt by flatteries: but the people that do **know** their God shall be strong, and do exploits" (Daniel 11:32).

ATTRIBUTES OF GOD

In order for us to truly know God, it helps us to understand his attributes. The attributes of God are revealed to us through his identity and through his activities. As we search the Scriptures, we find that God is engaged in activities that require specific attributes. There are many of these attributes, but for the purposes of our study, we will focus on three. The first attribute is "omnipresence." This means that God is everywhere all the time—all at the same time. One of the clearest pictures of this attribute comes from the Book of Psalms.

"If I ascend up into heaven, thou art there: if I make my bed in hell, behold, thou art there" (Psalm 139:8).

God exists in heaven, God exists in hell, and God exists everywhere in between. The reason that God is omnipresent is because he exists at the highest dimension. From his throne, it is possible for him to fill all other dimensions beneath his place of existence. The Bible is clear that God fills all in all.

"Which is his body, the fulness of him [Jesus} **that filleth all in all**" (Ephesians 1:23).

Another essential quality of God is the fact that he is "omniscient." This means that he is all-knowing. There is no knowledge that exists outside of the reach of God's comprehension. There is nothing that happens of which God is unaware. Nothing is hidden from his sight. This attribute of God is plainly revealed in the following passages.

"O lord, thou hast searched me, and known me. Thou knowest my downsitting and mine uprising, thou understandest my thought afar off. Thou compassest my path and my lying down, and art acquainted with all my ways. For there is not a word in my tongue, but, lo, O Lord, thou knowest it altogether. Thou hast beset me behind and before, and laid thine hand upon me. Such knowledge is too wonderful for me; it is high, I cannot attain unto it" (Psalm 139:1-6).

"The Lord looketh from heaven; he beholdeth all the sons of men. From the place of his habitation he looketh upon all the inhabitants of the earth. He fashioneth their hearts alike; he considereth all their works" (Psalm 33:13-15).

God is also "omnipotent." This means that it is in his nature to be all-powerful. There is no one greater than God. God is the Supreme Power from which all authority finds its inception. God is strong and mighty in battle. He is the Supreme Judge that executes justice throughout all of creation. His power is beyond expression, and all power in comparison to his is nothing more than counterfeit.

"For when God made promise to Abraham, because **he could swear by no greater**, he sware by himself" (Hebrews 6:13).

"Ah Lord God! behold, thou hast made the heaven and the earth by thy great power and stretched out arm, and **there is nothing too hard for thee**" (Jeremiah 32:17).

Sharing God's Attributes

As we begin to establish the identity of God, we must take into account that we are made one with him. Salvation in Jesus Christ results in the reception of the Holy Spirit into our spirit, making us one Spirit with God (1 Corinthians 6:17). This allows us to become a part of the spirit realm as an element of the very body of Christ. In other words, on higher dimensional planes, our spirits are actually comprising the body of Christ. As members of his body we gain access to all of his great and precious promises. This is because all of the promises of God are found in Christ.

"Whereby are given unto us exceeding **great and precious promises**: that by these ye might be partakers of the **divine nature**, having escaped the corruption that is in the world through lust" (2 Peter 1:4).

By way of these great and precious promises, we actually become partakers of the divine nature. The divine nature is God's nature. *Becoming a partaker of the divine nature involves taking part in the nature of God.* This idea is awkward at first, but as we grow into ever-deepening intimacy with God, we have no choice but to accept that we share his nature. Not only do we share his nature, we participate in his nature as well.

Consider the fact that God is omnipotent. There is nothing that he is not strong enough to do. When we are in Christ, we clearly participate in this attribute of God. As a result of his power and presence (at work in and through us), the Bible presents us with a profound passage. It straightforwardly declares that we can do ALL THINGS through Christ who strengthens us. The fact that God is spiritually joined to us allows us to participate in this element of his nature.

"I can do all things through Christ which strengtheneth me" (Philippians 4:13).

Furthermore, consider the fact that God is omniscient. There is nothing that God does not know. There is no level of understanding that he cannot comprehend. There is no truth that is not present in him. As a result of this quality, and the limits of our own feeble minds, God gives Christians access to his mind. The Bible actually states that, although no one can know the mind of the Lord that he may instruct him, we have been given the mind of Christ. We share in the omniscient nature of God as a result of his great and precious promises towards us!

"For who hath known the mind of the Lord, that he may instruct him? but **we have the mind of Christ**" (1 Corinthians 2:16).

We partake in every attribute that God has: plain and simple. Otherwise, the Bible would not say that we are partakers of the divine nature. Does this sound sacrilegious? Only to those who have not renewed their minds to what Jesus actually accomplished at his death, burial, and resurrection. Children take on the nature of their parents. As children of God (John 1:12), why should we expect that it should be any different for us? The essential concept to grasp when we approach this revelation is that it is by *his power and authority* that we partake of his nature. It is not according to our own power and authority. In moving into God's attribute of omnipresence, the pattern remains the same.

Allow me to preface this discussion by making something very clear. I *do not* believe that we are fully omnipresent. That would be ridiculous. What I am saying is that we *take part* in God's omnipresent nature. The Spirit of the Lord has the ability to take us to any place in the world or on any dimensional plane (in spirit). Frankly, he also has the ability to do this with our physical body as well (Acts 8:38–39), although this is much less common.

He has the ability to take us into future events, presently occurring situations we have no knowledge of, and also into past events (in spirit). This kind of activity is typically identified with the gifts of word of wisdom, word of knowledge, discerning of spirits, or more commonly, a combination of spiritual gifts at work all at once (1 Corinthians 12:8–10). The line between us partaking of the "omniscient" nature of God and the "omnipresent" nature of God is often blurred relative to these gifts. However, the important idea to grasp is that by the Spirit of the Lord we cease to be limited to the natural plane.

One testimony in particular stands out as a vivid example of this principle at work. A couple of individuals came to me for help. They were living in a house with a number of other family members. The father had become very depressed, and the grandmother never left the basement. In addition, odd things had begun to happen to them as they were growing closer to God. Their living situation had become very difficult for a number of reasons, and they found themselves in the midst of some pretty serious spiritual warfare.

As I proceeded to pray for them, I was able to look at a representation of their house in the spirit. I didn't go to their physical house to pray because it was in another state (geographically). As I was looking at this representation of their house while in prayer, I saw a spirit wrapped around the house like a wedding ring wrapped around a finger. I immediately understood that the physical house itself was in some form of covenant with the kingdom of darkness.

I began to pray according to what I saw. Immediately as I did this I could feel the resistance in the spirit realm. The method of the enemy's torment had been revealed to me. As I specifically addressed the issue in prayer, there was nowhere for the enemy to run. What occurred was an extremely powerful time of prayer as I broke the power of the covenant in the name and authority of Jesus Christ. This may sound fictitious and off-kilter to those who are unfamiliar with God working in this way. However, we must remember that even if we don't completely understand what's going on, the Bible says, "you shall know them by their fruit." So, what was the fruit? The father immediately came out of the depression he had been suffering from and the grandmother left the basement the next day. Furthermore, everyone started getting along better and the spiritual attack on these individuals lifted for a season. Talk about fruit!

The point I want make is in regards to how I was able to look at a spiritual representation of the house. I had never so much as seen their house in the natural. The question is: what enabled me to see the house and the spiritual element at work there? I submit to you that because I am a partaker of the divine nature, the Holy Spirit was able to show me the house in spirit, according to his attribute of omnipresence and/or omniscience. By the same means, it is just as acceptable that he could show me things going on in other countries, underground, underwater, and even in space. Not only *can* he do this, *he has done this.* The simple fact of the matter is that this is part of our inheritance in Christ: it belongs to us.

On another occasion, a woman told me that she had a dream that she was locked up in an underwater prison. Not only was she locked up in this prison, but so was her car, the promissory note for her house, as well as a number of other individuals. Since I knew what I was dealing with, I had the angels of the Lord escort her to the prison during our ministry session. Immediately (without leaving her body) she realized that she was at the underwater prison, as she had been escorted there by the angels of the Lord. There was a very angry spirit that was part alligator and part man that began to yell at her upon arrival. She heard him say, "I knew you were trouble! What have you done!?"

This spirit knew his time was up. I laughed before going into warfare. Frankly, I laughed about it afterwards, too: and so did she! Even God laughs at his enemies (Psalm 2). I've simply learned to laugh with him. As I prayed, she watched in the spirit as all of the prison doors were opened up and her house note, the part of her that was imprisoned there, and her car, were set all free. *Everyone else being held hostage by the prison was set free too.* This was mass deliverance. This is what I call a dimensional raid, and I do it all the time. The armies of heaven promptly demolished and exploded the entire underwater dimensional prison until nothing was left but a ruinous heap. All of the evil spirits employed by this dimensional prison were arrested and taken away for judgment. From beginning to end this leveling of the devil's territory took about 15 minutes. She was amazed at the fierceness of the angels of the Lord, in that the destruction was so fast and excessive that the spirits of the people being set free were actually scrambling to clear the facility because it was coming down so fast.

God can literally relocate our spirit according to his nature of omnipresence. He does this to allow for certain kinds of interactions. In other words, since God is everywhere all at once, he can transfer our unconscious element (our spirit) to anywhere in order to fulfill his purposes. A more exceptional picture of this concept at work occurs in the Book of Acts. This beautiful illustration is all too often ignored or brushed under the proverbial carpet. The story goes that as Paul was on one of his journeys, he had a vision of a man from Macedonia beckoning him to travel there.

"And a vision appeared to Paul in the night; There stood a man of Macedonia, and prayed him, saying, Come over into Macedonia, and help us" (Acts 16:9).

I never understood this passage fully until I had a peculiar experience. Someone very close to me was struggling deeply with a certain issue and was seeking help. Needless to say, this person was a Christian. As a good brother in Christ, I was praying for them. At this point in my life, I had become rather accustomed to the Lord's voice in prayer, but during this particular prayer session I began to hear a voice I wasn't familiar with. Comments were made regarding this person's situation that I knew were lies. They were the same lies that the person was struggling with, which is why they were in a battle in the first place!

I was thinking: *Why am I hearing the deceptions that this person is presently struggling with? This is not the Spirit of God!* That's when I saw that the speech was coming from this particular person's spirit. I was blown away. I was expecting the voice to be coming from a demon whispering into the person's ear or something along those lines. Instead, the person's spirit was the one doing the talking. I saw this as a sort of vision. I also saw some of the bondages that this individual was entwined with in the spirit realm.

That's when I realized what had happened. On this occasion, the Lord had actually allowed me to hear and see the communications of another person's spirit without the person being physically present. The purpose was to help me understand how to better minister to the individual both in person and in prayer. In order for this to occur, it required partaking of the omnipresent nature of God (in spirit). While we are not everywhere all at once, according to the will of God we can be anywhere at any time, meaning we are simply partaking of his nature.

LIVING BY THE SPIRIT

Part of growing up into maturity involves allowing our identity to fuse with God's identity. This is what the apostle referred to when he prayed for Christ to be formed within those at the Church of Galatia (Galatians 4:19). As Christ is formed within us, his nature gains greater dominance, allowing for it to be expressed through our lives more effectively. This carries with it indescribable benefits. For instance, as we fuse our identity into God's identity during times of deep prayer, it allows us to pray with almost perfect accuracy. As we flow with the Spirit, he can impart to us information about the spirit realm, past events, future events, and activities that are presently occurring of which we have no knowledge (in the natural).

Operating according to all of these spiritual benefits leads to a life defined by the Bible as "living after the spirit." Spiritual Christians are not Christians that follow "all the rules" so as to become modern-day Pharisees. Purity and holiness are by-products of their lifestyle. Spiritual Christians are the ones who are trained to operate according to realities found in higher dimensions. They are the ones who experience, interact with, and engage the spirit realm as citizens of the kingdom of God. I define the kingdom of God as the realm in which God is King. This realm exists in the third heaven and contains the dimensions, heavenly places, and spirits that are in submission to God's kingship. With this perspective in mind, truly living a "kingdom" lifestyle requires purposeful trans-dimensional activity.

Before proceeding further, I want to point out how the Book of Revelation was written. It wasn't a dream. It was the result of a man who spent time *in the Spirit*. It was the result of a man who practiced engaging higher dimensions, embracing the spirit above the flesh, and sharing in the attributes of God as a lifestyle. The entire book is the account of a spiritual experience revealing truths about the past, present, and future. The important point is how the writer begins his account. It all begins with a man who was willing to be *in the Spirit*. Where have you been living?

"**I was in the Spirit** on the Lord's day, and heard behind me a great voice, as of a trumpet" (Revelation 1:10).

CHAPTER 15

Touching on Parallel Dimensions

Early in this book I made the clear distinction between higher dimensions and parallel dimensions. We defined parallel dimensions with the example of two one-dimensional lines on a piece of paper. The paper, as a two-dimensional space, is able to theoretically house an infinite number of one-dimensional units. In this example, the one-dimensional units are parallel to each other, or *parallel dimensions*.

Since we understand that our three-dimensional world is contained by four-dimensional space, it begs the question: are there other three-dimensional worlds housed by that same four-dimensional space? Furthermore, if there are, what relevance would they have for us? In order to approach this issue we must deal with the concept of time.

TIME AND MULTIPLE TIMELINES

Time does not affect higher dimensions in the same way it impacts the physical world. God is not bound by time, meaning that the works of the Holy Spirit are not bound by time. God exists both inside and outside of time and looks at the entirety of world history at once. The Bible says of God that he knows the end from the beginning.

"Declaring the **end** from the **beginning**, and from ancient times the things that are not yet done, saying, My counsel shall stand, and I will do all my pleasure" (Isaiah 46:10).

When we begin to discuss time and its relevance in light of other dimensions, the conversation can easily become both confusing and discouraging. However, I believe that with the right approach, this issue will become both logical and fascinating to you. In our world, time does not exist in and of itself. According to Einstein's work, particularly the theory of relativity, scientists have long understood that what we call time is really best understood as space-time. In other words, time is inseparable from the space to which it is tied. If there were a separate three-dimensional space (or universe) than our own, it would have its own time tied to it. Thus, the topic of parallel dimensions requires the consideration of multiple timelines.

In certain types of science fiction stories, one will find an allusion to multiple timelines. In the world of make-believe, multiple timelines imply that multiple "copies" or "versions" of a person exist in alternate universes (parallel dimensions). However, in each universe, a slightly different sequence of events occurs. While a particular individual may get married in one universe, in another universe that marriage may never happen. In a third universe they may get married twice, and limiting potential universes to three, the person would get married three times in all. The question is, do parallel dimensions allow for fully independent chronologies?

CLARIFYING THE WORD *ONCE*

Few would argue that the greatest work of God involved sending Jesus Christ to die for our sins and to redeem men and women back to himself. Everything in the Bible centers on the work of Jesus Christ. All that occurred prior to his death, burial, and resurrection points forward to it. All that occurred after his death, burial, and resurrection points back to it. This event is the single most important work of God as identified by the Bible. It reveals God's character, motive, and purpose for man.

"For God so loved the world, that he gave his only begotten Son, that whosoever believeth in him should not perish, but have everlasting life" (John 3:16).

Just because the operation of parallel dimensions as defined by science fiction is possible, it doesn't necessarily require this possibility to be true. As a matter of fact, based on the death, burial, and resurrection of Jesus, I don't believe it is possible for it to be true (in the way science fiction has explained it). If there were another copy of me present in a parallel dimension, that copy would need the redemption of Jesus just as much as the copy of me that is writing this book. For that dimension to be parallel to ours, it would require it to have also experienced the fall of man. This would require Jesus to experience his death, burial, and resurrection in every existing parallel dimension. Basic logic forces us to accept that he'd have to die more than once in order to do this. According to the following passages, this is impossible.

"For Christ also hath **once** suffered for sins, the just for the unjust, that he might bring us to God, being put to death in the flesh, but quickened by the Spirit" (1 Peter 3:18).
"For in that he died, he died unto sin **once**: but in that he liveth, he liveth unto God" (Romans 6:10).
"Who [Jesus] needeth not daily, as those high priests, to offer up sacrifice, first for his own sins, and then for the people's: for this he did **once**, when he offered up himself" (Hebrews 7:27).

Since Jesus died only once, we must accept that whatever exists parallel to this dimension does not require an independent atoning sacrifice of God. It is tempting to ponder the thought, *maybe the Bible is actually explaining that Jesus died only once in our dimension*. The problem is that the Bible simply says he died <u>once</u>—period. In other words, I would not find another copy of myself in another dimension that needed the redemption of Jesus Christ in that dimension. Since Jesus died only once, this would mean that either I just so happen to be the lucky copy of myself; or more realistically—that I am the only original copy of myself.

A BASE TIMELINE

This leads us to the concept of a base timeline. In other words, there is only one official timeline that actually manifests. It is on this one timeline that you and I exist, and it is on this one timeline that Jesus died in order to redeem us back to God. This timeline is upheld by the word of God. What is written in the word of God cannot be changed. Jesus is clear that not one jot or tittle would pass from the law till all be fulfilled.

"For verily I say unto you, Till heaven and earth pass, one jot or one tittle shall in no wise pass from the law, till all be fulfilled" (Matthew 5:18).

No part of human history recorded by the Bible can be changed. Furthermore, nothing recorded by the Bible pertaining to the future can be changed. Bible prophecy will be fulfilled. This helps us to treat the discussion of multiple timelines with a logical foundation. Do multiple timelines exist? Not as fully independent chronologies. Biblically speaking, there can only be one base timeline. This is the same timeline that you and I exist on, and it is also the same timeline that Jesus died on. While this may clear up some confusion on the issue, it is certainly not the end of the discussion. It is only the beginning.

POTENTIAL REALITIES

I actually believe that there are different kinds of parallel dimensions. I will plainly state that the function of some of these dimensions are outside of the parameters of this book, but relate to things I have dealt with in working with those who have been part of secret government and/or New World Order projects. What I can say is that at least one type of parallel dimension seems to be clearly explained by the Bible. *These are parallel dimensions that contain potential realities that simultaneously exist yet do not necessarily manifest.* I know that this may sound like quite a mouthful, but before you put the book down, allow me to explain this thought. Take the evidence with a grain of salt, and understand that, like you, I do not have all the answers. This is simply how I believe things might work as of the printing of this book.

I am under the impression that *potential (or possible) realities* exist parallel to our timeline. These potential realities are what occult prophets and seers like Nostradamus and Edgar Cayce looked at. Likewise, they are what Satan and his army of evil spirits look at. These are our parallel dimensions. If we were able to cross four-dimensional space, I believe we might encounter these potential realities and even have the ability to interact with them. We could almost think about them like dream worlds. They may look and feel real, but unless they manifest into the base timeline, they would simply remain <u>possible</u> realities. This would make them pictures and illustrations of what could be or what may have been. They would be the *expression* of the results of choices either not taken or not yet taken.

Regarding this type of parallel dimension, this means that if I were able to cross four-dimensional space and find a copy of myself, that copy would be a picture or illustration of me in light of certain decisions made.

It would not actually be me; it would not possess a spirit, and it would basically exist as a "movie" or "recording" of me under those specific circumstances. In order to accept this concept it requires a couple of basic paradigms to be in operation. It requires us to believe that not only do people have the ability to exercise genuine choice, but that God has created provision for choices to be made (which would have to exist as potential realities). By proving that genuine choice has the ability to be made by humans, I believe that it validates the possibility for this perspective to be true.

THE REALITY OF CHOICE

Let's take a step back and consider an example. Waking up in the morning can be difficult sometimes. This is particularly true when I have had a late night or I know that I have a long, hard day ahead of me. On these difficult mornings I have two choices. I can either stay in bed or I can get up and be productive. Does the Holy Spirit personally show up and yank me out of bed as if I were some sort of robot? No. I have a choice, and my choice will either be in line with God's will or it won't. This is called free will. We are to prove God's good and perfect will by agreeing with it in both thought and deed.

"And be not conformed to this world: but be ye transformed by the renewing of your mind, that ye may prove what is that good, and acceptable, and perfect, will of God" (Romans 12:2).

Every morning that I wake up and choose to be productive, the potential reality of staying in bed does not manifest. However, prior to my decision, it exists as a possible future. Only once I make a decision does the possible future cease to be a possible future. Instead it gives way to manifested history. However, I believe that somewhere in the spirit realm (in spaces parallel to our dimension), one can actually look at and see that possible future. Even once a decision has been made, I still believe that one can look at what could have happened. This would not exist as a fully independent timeline, but simply as a fragment realm displaying what may be or what could have been.

When God made his covenant with Israel in the Book of Deuteronomy, he actually presented them with two possible futures. Then he said that _they_ would have to choose. While we know that Israel chose to rebel against God time after time, God made provision for an incredibly blessed national destiny. The only requirement was that they would have to _choose_ to be faithful. I believe that God, knowing the ultimate decisions that the nation of Israel would make, still made provision for different decisions. In other words, we have an answer for why the Bible declares that the Lord forms light and creates evil and darkness. He, as Creator, creates all possible decisions beforehand in order to allow for the reality of choice.

"I form the light, and create darkness: I make peace, and create evil: I the Lord do all these things" (Isaiah 45:7).

He does this to prove his justice and fairness. In respect to Israel, if the possibility for their prosperous future didn't exist as a potential reality, then God would not have presented it as such.

"And it **shall** come to pass, **if thou shalt hearken diligently unto the voice of the Lord thy God,** to observe and to do all his commandments which I command thee this day, that the Lord thy God will set thee on high above all nations of the earth: And all these blessings shall come on thee, and overtake thee, if thou shalt hearken unto the voice of the Lord thy God.

Blessed shalt thou be in the city, and blessed shalt thou be in the field" (Deuteronomy 28:1–3).

Students of the Bible know that Israel spent much of its time swaying between obedience and disobedience. Their dominant choice was disobedience. Therefore, much of their history does not bear out the manifestation of the blessings stated in the first part of Deuteronomy 28. Instead, their history bears out the second part of Deuteronomy 28, which lists one curse after the other. This cursed potential reality manifested according to the choices the nation made. This reality was not God's choice for the nation, it was the nation's choice for itself. God simply made provision for this reality to be chosen.

"But it **shall** come to pass, **if thou wilt not hearken unto the voice of the Lord thy God,** to observe to do all his commandments and his statutes which I command thee this day; that all these curses shall come upon thee, and overtake thee: Cursed shalt thou be in the city, and cursed shalt thou be in the field. Cursed shall be thy basket and thy store. Cursed shall be the fruit of thy body, and the fruit of thy land, the increase of thy kine, and the flocks of thy sheep. Cursed shalt thou be when thou comest in, and cursed shalt thou be when thou goest out" (Deuteronomy 28:15–19).

I recognize that there are some reading this book who harbor the preconceived notion that choice is simply an illusion. In other words, all things are predestined and everything that will be—*will be*. They believe that to think that we have a choice is to be simple-minded. Since God knows everything before it happens, these individuals believe that destiny, calling, election, or whatever else one may want to call it, is the overriding factor in what comes of a person's life.

While there are powerful truths to reap regarding the biblical concepts of "calling" and "election," they cannot be defined as the overriding factor regarding what comes of a person's life. The following verse absolutely refutes this paradigm in no uncertain words. God, pictured as speaking through Moses to the nation of Israel, told them that the choice was *theirs* to make. If choice was an illusion, God would not present choice as the most powerful deciding factor regarding the destiny of the nation. *Israel was called and elected to be God's chosen nation.* However, the most powerful factor deciding its national destiny was actually the choices made by the people comprising it.

"I call heaven and earth to record this day against you, that I have set before you life and death, blessing and cursing: therefore **choose life**, that both thou and thy seed may live" (Deuteronomy 30:19).

When it comes to what manifests on our timeline, we must understand that it has a lot to do with the choices we make. In other words, just because God may know our choices in advance, it doesn't mean that he makes them for us. This passage is very clear that God set both life and death before Israel. God created two potential realities regarding the destiny of the nation. The first was life, and the second was death. Both of these potential realities existed simultaneously, but the reality that manifested was the reality that the nation chose with its actions. As the historical record bears out, the nation predominantly operated under the curse. However, when the nation went through reform, deliverance, and restoration, the reality that it manifested would change to the blessing. This could be described as the nation changing its frequency.

Multiple Frequencies as an Illustration of Parallel Dimensions

Most of us are familiar with a useful invention known as the radio. A radio is designed to tune in to invisible forces that travel through the air known as frequencies. For us in America, we are primarily familiar with AM tuning, FM tuning, and shortwave radio. In order to operate a radio, one must first connect it to a power source (batteries, electrical outlet, etc.). Once it has power, the radio can then be used to tune into a specific frequency. The speakers on the device will play the sounds carried by whatever frequency the device is tuned to.

While none of the frequencies "see" each other or are "aware" of each other, they all exist. Moreover, they all exist simultaneously. Although a radio only tunes into one broadcast frequency at a time, all radio broadcast frequencies remain simultaneously available. These frequencies are all contained by the same air and atmosphere. The moment a decision is made to tune in to a different frequency, the sound that the radio plays is changed accordingly. This is how a radio functions.

Now we will relate this concept to our developing comprehension of parallel dimensions. We will begin by breaking down the radio technology into fundamental elements. These elements are the power source, the radio itself, the frequencies, and the air or atmosphere. Four-dimensional space is like the atmosphere. Just like the atmosphere contains multiple radio frequencies, four-dimensional space contains multiple three-dimensional spaces. Therefore, the three-dimensional spaces are like the frequencies.

The radio is like the base timeline that we have defined. There is only one device, and at any given time it will only play *one* of a plethora of possible frequencies. There is only *one* base timeline. Only *one* of a plethora of possible realities will actually manifest on it. This timeline is upheld by the word of God, its proverbial power source (Hebrews 1:3). This makes the word of God like the battery or electrical outlet that actually powers the radio.

In the same way that many radio frequencies exist simultaneously, many potential realities exist simultaneously as well. Instead of existing as waves, they exist as parallel dimensions. Once they are "tuned into," so to speak, they will manifest on our timeline. When we change the frequency that we are tuned into, our decisions will cause a different reality to manifest. The power of human choice resides at the center of this concept.

This brings us back to our example from the nation of Israel. The nation of Israel was allegorically tuned into 66.6 FM "The Curse" for a majority of its history. However, there were brief windows of time during which it was tuned into 77.7 FM "The Blessing." The choices made by the nation of Israel determined whether they received life or death. Both realities existed simultaneously at all times, but the one that was chosen by the people was the one that manifested. It is my belief that this is the relevance of at least one type of parallel dimension in light of a single base timeline.

The Importance of Decision

So, where do we go from here? I believe that the most powerful lesson we can glean from this discussion is the *importance of decision*. In other words, the realities that manifest are always going to be the result of the decisions that people make. Truth be told, even unfulfilled biblical prophecy boils down to a foretelling of the results of people's decisions as directed and influenced by the providence of God. As humans created in God's image, we have the divine ability to call forth the realities that we experience. This is why we need to get in agreement with God and begin to call forth realities in line with his kingdom. We are to replace the realities of this fallen world with the realities of God's dimension, otherwise known as his kingdom. Hence, the Lord's Prayer:

"And he said unto them, When ye pray, say, Our Father which art in heaven, Hallowed be thy name. **Thy kingdom come. Thy will be done, as in heaven, so in earth**" (Luke 11:2).

Revisiting the Conscious, Subconscious, and Unconscious

If you have tracked with me this far you are probably thinking that this is some great information, but you may be curious as to how understanding these things will produce a positive impact in your life. The goal of this book is to target paradigm. If I wanted to give you twelve steps to freedom from alcohol addiction I would have referred you to Alcoholics Anonymous. My goal isn't to give you steps to a new and better you. The goal is to awaken you to a new way of viewing and processing everything around you. I want you begin to view your life, this world, and God—not with the paradigm you've had—but with one that is closer to that which is held by your Creator. As you allow the things I have written in this book to sink into your heart, it will change the way your subconscious processes everything. When that happens, the change will come all by itself.

One of the most powerful lessons I have learned is that our different non-physical components are intended to interact with different realms of existence. Our soul, which is our mind, will, and emotions, is designed to deal with this world and the realm of the first heaven. Our conscious mind processes information on a carnal level. It learns, interacts, and responds according to the events that occur in the first heaven, which is our three-dimensional world. While it can learn, deal with, and process all kinds of information, very little of what enters our conscious mind will become part of our subconscious, or belief system. Our will and emotions are also designed to operate on this plane of existence. The soul is designed to interact with the physical dimension.

Our heart (or subconscious) actually deals with what our life will manifest. As we formerly discussed, the Bible is clear that, "as a man thinks in his heart, so is he." Reprogramming our hearts can cause us to experience a whole new set of realities. When we begin to allow heavenly programs to operate in our hearts, we will walk out into a supernatural life of victory, fulfillment, joy, peace, and power. When we begin to allow programs based on fear and trauma to operate in our hearts, we will walk out into depression, poverty, wickedness, shame, and hopelessness. Thus, it can be said that our hearts allow us to interact with parallel dimensions. *The heart of the individual is like the radio that tunes in to a frequency because its program will ultimately be the source of the decision-making patterns in an individual's life.*

Lastly, our spirit is designed to interact with higher dimensions. When the Bible says we have been raised up and seated with Christ in heavenly places, it is referencing the activity and location of our spirit (Ephesians 2:6). Since we operate on the highest dimension with Christ, we must also understand that we simultaneously exist across all lower dimensions. In light of this, the activity of our spirit is often far beyond our ability to frame with three-dimensional concepts. Our spiritual nature is trans-dimensional and our spiritual experiences are being processed by our unconscious mind, which is located in our spirit. However, as we renew our mind to spiritual things and allow God to program our hearts according to heavenly paradigms, we will begin to operate according to the Spirit as opposed to the flesh. This is God's goal for all Christians.

CHAPTER 16

Regions of Captivity

At this point we are ready to move into a discussion on "regions of captivity." These places of bondage, captivity, and torment are found in the spirit realm and unfortunately, most Christians have no idea regarding what the term even means. I have purposefully saved this discussion until now because understanding higher dimensions and the trans-dimensional nature of the spirit are prerequisites for attaining a firm grasp on this topic.

The basic concept is that, since our spirit is trans-dimensional, it can be put in bondage on the dimensional levels where the kingdom of darkness can access it. Some people think that a human spirit redeemed by God cannot be touched by the enemy, but this is an oversimplification. The part of our spirit that houses the Holy Spirit cannot be touched, but that is only *part* of our spirit. Furthermore, this has no application to the soul, which we have already defined as being entirely different from the spirit.

CAN THE ENEMY TOUCH CHRISTIANS?

"We know that whosoever is born of God sinneth not; but he that is begotten of God keepeth himself, and that wicked one toucheth him not" (1 John 5:18).

There is no question that this verse says that the "wicked one touches him not." However, right before this statement, John writes that whosoever is born of God doesn't sin. *The problem is that Christians sin.* As a matter of fact, earlier in this same book John writes that, "If we say we have no sin, we deceive ourselves, and the truth is not in us" (1 John 1:8). So, how does this make sense? How can we properly exegete what John is telling us? The truth is that there is a part of us, namely the part of our spirit that contains the Holy Spirit (1 Corinthians 6:17), that cannot sin and cannot be touched. However, this is clearly not our entire spirit. How do we know? The Apostle Paul outlines in no uncertain terms that we (him included) must cleanse ourselves of all filthiness of the flesh and <u>spirit</u>. Therefore, even part of the Christian spirit can have filthiness (or bondage).

"Having therefore these promises, dearly beloved**, let <u>us</u> cleanse ourselves from all filthiness of the flesh and <u>spirit</u>**, perfecting holiness in the fear of God" (2 Corinthians 7:1).

This leads us to understand that there really are different levels of bondage. Since we have already defined the spirit and soul as separate elements of our non-physical nature, we must understand that attacks and bondages can form on both levels. The enemy can attack our mind, will, and emotions, and under certain circumstances, can even afflict our spirit. In addition he can use fear, trauma, negative experiences, and so forth to program our heart according to his paradigms. He truly stops at nothing to steal, kill, and destroy (John 10:10). This is why many ministries are unsuccessful in helping people who have certain problems. They don't understand how to implement God's provision to set people free from the various types of afflictions that the devil is vaulting against them. The most unfortunate part is that, in my experience, many don't want to understand.

The Unforgiving Servant

In any case, we are now ready to discuss regions of captivity. In essence, this occurs when our spirit comes in contact with fourth-dimensional locations like hell and the pit. Not only do our spirits come in contact with these places, but our spirits can be bound up in them. This won't usually occur unless there is generational sin and/or curses at work to allow for it (Deuteronomy 5:9). Conversely, it may also occur if the person is engaging in willful sin. In the parable of the unforgiving servant, a servant's lord forgives him of a huge debt. Afterwards, this servant finds a man who owes him relatively little. He has the man thrown in prison instead of also forgiving the debt. When his lord finds out (the lord representing our Father in heaven) this is what is written:

"Then his lord, after that he had called him, said unto him, O thou wicked servant, I forgave thee all that debt, because thou desiredst me: Shouldest not thou also have had compassion on thy fellowservant, even as I had pity on thee? And his lord was wroth, and **delivered him to the tormentors**, till he should pay all that was due unto him. **So likewise shall my heavenly Father do also unto you**, if ye from your hearts forgive not every one his brother their trespasses" (Matthew 18:32–35).

Jesus is clear that sin such as unforgiveness will lead us into spiritual torment *even under the New Covenant.* Until the portion of our spirit that is bound in these places is freed by Jesus, we will continue to have unexplainable oppression in our lives. The implications are that not only will we come under demonic oppression, but also under oppression that results from adverse spiritual environments. Like I have already illustrated, this can be just as true for the Christian as for the unredeemed individual, because only a portion of our spirit remains untouchable.

Dimensional Imprisonment or Allegory?

There is little question that this is new information for many people. For this reason we are going to take some time to look at other scriptural evidence of this fact. The next passage we will be looking at comes from the Book of Psalms. The problem is that for most of us, we write this Psalm off as allegory because we don't have the knowledge or understanding to accept what it is saying at face value. As you will see, the Bible couldn't be much clearer.

"O lord God of my salvation, I have cried day and night before thee: Let my prayer come before thee: incline thine ear unto my cry; For my soul is full of troubles: and my life draweth nigh unto the grave. **I am counted with them that go down into the pit**: I am as a man that hath no strength: Free among the dead, like the slain that lie in the grave, whom thou rememberest no more: and they are cut off from thy hand. **Thou hast laid me in the lowest pit, in darkness, in the deeps**" (Psalm 88:1–6).

In verse six of this Psalm, the writer, who was very much alive in the physical sense, stated that he had been laid in the lowest pit, in darkness, in the deeps. This means that he recognized that he had been placed into an adverse spiritual environment. The pit is the location of the fallen angel Apollyon, for goodness' sake (Revelation 9:11)! So how did this happen? The answer is that his spirit had come in contact with these realms and he felt the affliction that they imposed upon him. He was actually imprisoned by them. Unlike the majority of people this happens to, he had a revelation of what his unconscious was experiencing. He was able to relate this experience as a lament, and thereby give us a revelation of just what is possible in the spirit realm. When the prophecy of Jesus went forth, the agenda to proclaim liberty to the captives and the opening of the prison to them that are bound was first and foremost spiritual.

"The Spirit of the Lord GOD is upon me; because the LORD hath anointed me to preach good tidings unto the meek; he hath sent me to bind up the brokenhearted, to proclaim liberty to the captives, and **the opening of the prison to them that are bound**" (Isaiah 61:1).

Some individuals I have spoken with have made claims that, looking back, made me wonder if this was their problem. Have you ever heard someone said, "Why do I need to go to hell, I'm already there"? I personally believe that many people who would say this are partially right. There has been a dimensional overlap of hell, or the pit, upon their spirit, and while they don't specifically know what's happening to them—in some ways they do. Even though we remain largely unaware of what our unconscious mind experiences, we will still experience the impact. Just like our physical body can be held captive by dungeons and prisons, the same can happen in the spirit.

"I the Lord have called thee in righteousness, and will hold thine hand, and will keep thee, and give thee for a covenant of the people, for a light of the Gentiles; To open the blind eyes, **to bring out the prisoners from the prison, and them that sit in darkness out of the prison house**" (Isaiah 42:6–7).

MINISTERING TO THE REAL WORLD

I remember praying with a certain friend on one occasion. He was having a problem in that he often felt distant from God. He felt as though he had a spiritual haze or barrier blocking him from going deeper in his faith. The incredible part was that this friend had attended the same Bible school as I had. He had even led worship before thousands of people. He was saved, he had received the gift of the Holy Spirit (so he spoke in tongues), and he had also been baptized in water.

In the minds of some, there was no reason he should have any major spiritual problems at this point in his life. If you are like me, you have probably heard arguments like, "Jesus became a curse for us (Galatians 3:13) and where the light dwells there can be no darkness. Therefore once we have Jesus we can't be cursed or have any spiritual problems unless they are entirely external." Unfortunately, this theology has no effectiveness in the real world. My friend, along with many other Christians who have found themselves in the situation he was in, still have spiritual problems. Telling them they "shouldn't have problems" solves nothing.

As we entered into prayer, I released my faith to operate in the gift of discerning of spirits. Sure enough, I was looking at a picture of his spiritual situation. I saw his spirit standing on a high place overlooking something like a city. There was some kind of amber case surrounding him. It blocked him from his surroundings and blocked his surroundings from him. As I continued to look at it, I almost felt like it was composed of some sort of (spiritual) glass. I then knew that I was looking at his problem.

I felt the Holy Spirit communicate to me that this barrier needed to be broken. So I prayed and called upon angels to come and cause this barrier to be shattered. Angels showed up and obeyed, because angels hearken unto the voice of the word of the Lord (Psalm 103:20). When my speech is in line with God's will *I am the voice* and *the words in my mouth qualify as the word of the Lord*. This means that the angels will hearken unto me (and you, too!). When the angels shattered the spiritual object, my friend practically collapsed on the floor. I know it was entirely spiritual because at the time that this happened, I was praying for him from the other side of the room. I was not laying hands on him, meaning it would have been impossible for me to physically push him off balance.

While this does not illustrate that his spirit was actually overlapped by the pit, it illustrates the concept I am trying to communicate. His spiritual environment, at least on the dimension in which I was viewing it, was in bondage. He wasn't possessed by a demon, he was simply afflicted by existing in a spiritual environment contrary to the freedom that Jesus purchased for him. As I prayed and enforced the freedom that Jesus purchased for him, the works of God manifested in his life.

Addressing the Objections

For those who would argue that, "Jesus became a curse for us (Galatians 3:13) so we can't have spiritual problems," or "light and darkness cannot dwell together, therefore Christians cannot be demonized or imprisoned in spiritual environments," I want you to know that I believe that your objections are warranted. However, I do not believe that they are correct. In order to prove this we will begin in the Book of Acts. When Philip went preaching in the Book of Acts, he had a powerful encounter with a sorcerer named Simon. In light of the power that Philip was demonstrating, Simon had a revelation that Jesus was the true God. The result was that Simon got saved and baptized in water.

"But when they believed Philip preaching the things concerning the kingdom of God, and the name of Jesus Christ, they were baptized, both men and women. **Then Simon himself believed also: and when he was baptized, he continued with Philip**, and wondered, beholding the miracles and signs which were done" (Acts 8:12–13).

Simon was saved by grace through faith in Jesus Christ (Ephesians 2:8). Furthermore, he had been baptized according to the commandment of Jesus (Matthew 28:19). This means that he was covered by the blood of

Jesus and declared to be the righteousness of God in Christ (2 Corinthians 5:21). However, he was still in bondage! After the apostles in Jerusalem heard that the city of Samaria (where Simon lived) had received the word of God, they sent Peter and John. They went there to impart the gift of the Spirit, otherwise known as the baptism of the Holy Spirit (Acts 1:8, Acts 8:15–17). This is an inheritance of the believer that (most often) comes subsequent to salvation.

When Simon saw that through the laying on of hands the Holy Spirit was given, he offered the apostles money for the gift. In other words, he sinned. He had received Jesus Christ, he had been baptized in water, and he had spent some time following Philip. After all of this he still stumbled and sinned. This wasn't the end of his world because the Bible is clear that when we sin, we simply need to repent so that we will be cleansed of all unrighteousness (1 John 1:9). The problem for Simon was that this act of sin was the result of spiritual bondage that had yet to be dealt with. While part of his spirit was completely redeemed, another part remained in bondage. He was still in the gall of bitterness and in the bonds (or chains) of iniquity. How do we know? It was by the unction and revelation of the Holy Spirit that Peter spoke the following words to him.

"But Peter said unto him, Thy money perish with thee, because thou hast thought that the gift of God may be purchased with money. Thou hast neither part nor lot in this matter: for thy heart is not right in the sight of God. Repent therefore of this thy wickedness, and pray God, if perhaps the thought of thine heart may be forgiven thee. **For I perceive that thou art in the gall of bitterness, and in the <u>bond of iniquity</u>**" (Acts 8:20–23).

Just like Simon, Christians can be in spiritual bondage, chains, and prisons subsequent to salvation. These spiritual issues will lead to sin and if they aren't dealt with properly, can destroy our ability to walk out our faith long-term. They can and will cause us to backslide. They can and will bring destruction into our lives. The question is: how does this make sense if Jesus became a curse for us?

"Christ hath redeemed us from the curse of the law, being made a curse for us: for it is written, Cursed is every one that hangeth on a tree" (Galatians 3:13).

When Jesus became a curse for us he *purchased the right* for us to be completely free of all curses relative to the law. This grants provision for freedom, but we must receive his provision by faith. The reality of our freedom exists in the third heaven, but that reality must be enforced throughout the second heaven before it truly impacts our lives. This same principle applies to divine healing. The Bible clearly says that by the stripes of Jesus we were healed (1 Peter 2:24). Do Christians still get sick? Of course. The provision for our healing was purchased by Jesus, and the reality of our healing exists in the third heaven, but it must be enforced in the lower dimensions by faith.

For those who say that spiritual problems are impossible for the Christian because "where the light is there can be no darkness," it helps to take a look at what the Bible actually says. There is no question that God has called us out of darkness and into light.

"But ye are a chosen generation, a royal priesthood, an holy nation, a peculiar people; that ye should shew forth the praises of him who hath **called you out of darkness into his marvellous light**" (1 Peter 2:9).

Furthermore, the Bible is clear that the darkness doesn't comprehend the light.

"And the light shineth in darkness; and the darkness comprehended it not" (John 1:5).

However, what the Bible doesn't say is that a redeemed spirit cannot have any element of darkness. It doesn't say the heart cannot be deceived, and it certainly doesn't say the mind of the Christian cannot be corrupted. To the contrary, the following verses speak the exact opposite of these flawed conclusions.

"He that saith he is in the light, and hateth his brother, **is in darkness even until now**" (1 John 2:9).

"Take heed therefore that **the light which is in thee be not darkness**" (Luke 11:35).

"Then Jesus said unto them, Yet a little while is the light with you. **Walk while ye have the light, lest darkness come upon you**: for he that walketh in darkness knoweth not whither he goeth" (John 12:35).

"**The heart is deceitful** above all things, and desperately wicked: who can know it?" (Jeremiah 17:9).

"To the end **he may stablish your hearts unblameable** in holiness before God, even our Father, at the coming of our Lord Jesus Christ with all his saints" (1 Thessalonians 3:13).

"But I fear, lest by any means, as the serpent beguiled Eve through his subtilty, **so your minds should be corrupted** from the simplicity that is in Christ" (2 Corinthians 11:3).

According to the verses above, we learn quite a bit. First of all, we learn that the Christian who harbors hatred against their brother is in darkness. We can say that we embrace the light, that we believe in the light, that we have the light, but to harbor hatred is to harbor darkness. This is absolutely *possible* for the Christian. I have met countless Christians who have admitted to hating others (many times for reasons that are well warranted according to the flesh). This act keeps them in darkness until they forgive the offense and release the hatred and anger they are harboring. Just because a person goes through this process subsequent to salvation doesn't mean they aren't saved. It simply means that they are still partly in the darkness.

The Bible goes on to say that we cannot allow the light in us to become darkness. It follows that if we don't walk while we have the light, darkness can come upon us. The clear exegesis of these passages communicates one thing: that while we have the light of Jesus, we can knowingly (and at times unknowingly) embrace the darkness. How the argument "light and darkness cannot dwell together and therefore true Christians cannot have spiritual problems" can possibly be used as an acceptable objection is beyond me. It truly makes no sense. This takes us right back to the verse that we have looked at in previous chapters. We must cleanse ourselves of the filthiness of the flesh and spirit.

"Therefore, since these [great] promises are ours, beloved, let us cleanse ourselves from everything that contaminates *and* defiles body and spirit, and bring [our] consecration to completeness in the [reverential] fear of God" (2 Corinthians 7:1 AMPC).

Beyond the spiritual element, we also learn that the heart is deceitful, and that our hearts must be *established* as blameless before God. This means that a blameless heart condition isn't automatic; it is a process. We must willfully submit to this process in order to see our hearts established in holiness before God. We must allow the spirit of God to reprogram our subconscious by writing onto the fleshy tables of our hearts (2 Corinthians 3:3). We have formerly defined this as the process by which we allow God to reprogram our subconscious according to heavenly paradigms.

Furthermore, our minds can be corrupted. This is why we must continually renew our minds according to the word of God (Romans 12:2). While most Christians are willing to admit that the devil can corrupt the soul, I believe it's worth repeating here anyway. I want to make it very clear that except for the part of our spirit that contains the Holy Spirit, the enemy can touch, imprison, and demonize us when we are not enforcing the victory of Jesus Christ. This may not be a popular message, but if we are not willing to accept this, we will not be effective ministers to a lost and dying world. Our dismissal of truth will limit God's ability to use us. When we consider the whole counsel of the word of God we must conclude that freedom isn't automatic for the Christian. We have the provision for it, but we must receive it and enforce it by faith.

VISIONS OF ABADDON

Let us now take a look at another testimony that speaks directly to the concept outlined by Psalm 88. This testimony comes from the book *Regions of Captivity* by Dr. Ana Mendez Ferrell. The entire situation transpired as a vision the author experienced during a prayer session. The vision took her to a place in Abaddon (which means the place of destruction or the pit). The account is as follows:

> On another occasion, I had an experience that left me perplexed for a long time. Another servant of God in the United States approached me with severe financial problems. His father had been a military man and was in several wars. God does not call anyone to serve Him and then keep them in poverty. God is good and takes care of His servants.
>
> I began to pray until God showed me the region where he was captive. He was in Abaddon. I did not see the same

fortress I had seen before; this time it was a valley. A powerful angel appeared to lead me inside this vision.

I saw an enormous bloody plain with body parts strewn all around. The scene shocked me at first, but the presence of God's powerful messenger encouraged me. We walked for a while until we saw a gigantic demon. His image is still etched in my memory. He had enormous claws and growled thunderously. He was around 200 feet tall and would thrust his hands into a multitude of men clutching dozens of them at a time. Then he squeezed so hard they fell into pieces to the ground. This happened over and over again. He was between beast and man and was seated upon a mountain of incalculable riches.

The angel said this demon was *the Slaughterer*. The United States sold their children for money in the Vietnam War: The war involved lots of money and many young Americans died. The angelic messenger said this gave the demon the right to destroy and steal the riches of a nation.

The angel instructed me to hide behind his wings. We stealthily approached, careful not to let the demon see us as we came to the opening between his parted legs. Once inside the mountain of riches, we made our way through a tunnel of gold. This led to the minister's father in a dungeon. The man was hugging an enormous treasure that he jealously guarded, but could not use because he was captive. Under the direction of the Holy Spirit, I told the man to ask forgiveness for having participated in the war. He humbly asked forgiveness and gave us his treasure. In the same cell was his son; we removed them from there and since that time he has prospered."[34]

The idea that someone could have their spiritual eyes opened by the spirit of God to the extent that they become acutely aware of situations and environments in the spirit realm may be new information for some. However, this is simply part of the inheritance that we have in Christ. When God said that we would reign in life through Christ (1 Corinthians 5:17), that rule was intended to extend beyond the physical plane, and span into the higher dimensions. Walking in the fullness of this revelation takes us far beyond the limitations of the flesh and allows us to more effectively minister the will of God to this world. Why else would God say our war is not with flesh and blood but against principalities and powers (Ephesians 6:12) if we were to limit our understanding of our battles to the flesh?

Wrapping it Up

The important thing to take away from this chapter is the understanding that our spirit can exist in different types of spiritual environments, and depending on our circumstances, some of them can be contrary to God's will for our lives. Getting free of these environments can often happen by practicing the basic tenets of the faith like praying, repenting, reading the Bible, fasting, tithing, and so forth. In certain situations, it may be necessary to have others, who have the ability to discern these things, pray with us. Whatever the case may be, as long as we are willing to faithfully seek God for all that he has for us, he will bring us the freedom we need and provide all of the resources necessary. As it is written of Jesus:

"The Spirit of the Lord GOD is upon me; because the LORD hath anointed me to preach good tidings unto the meek; he hath sent me to bind up the brokenhearted, to proclaim liberty to the captives, and the opening of the prison to them that are bound" (Isaiah 61:1).

CHAPTER 17

Water Spirits

Earlier in this book, I mentioned that there were angelic spirits of the water. I then mentioned that I saw these spirits in heaven, and that their purpose was to go forth and destroy the wickedness in underwater places. This is very new information for many people. Most Christians can grasp the fact that there are spirits and a spirit realm, but the idea that spirits could be specifically associated with the sea is a major stretch. However, in order to set this chapter off in the right direction, we'll establish that, according to Scripture, there is at least one spirit (angel) of the waters. This will serve as an indisputable foundational truth for this chapter.

"And I heard the **angel of the waters** say, Thou art righteous, O Lord, which art, and wast, and shalt be, because thou hast judged thus" (Revelation 16:5).

The focus of this book is not to systematically expound on this largely unaddressed topic. Therefore, this chapter will simply provide enough insight to overcome the objections of the skeptic. My goal will be to set a biblical foundation that will allow you as the reader to begin your own exploration of the issue if you so desire. Wickedness in underwater places is real, and it is something that we need to be aware of.

A Revelatory Dream

Before I begin pulling this concept from the Scriptures, I want to introduce this topic from a personal testimony. One of my first encounters with evil water spirits came in a dream I had. The dream picked up as I and three other guys jumped off a cliff high up on a mountain. There were ledges that jutted out from the mountain as we began to fall. It happened that we would smack down on them hard, and then roll off to the next ledge, smacking down again. We finally got to the bottom of this mountain and realized that we'd all survived. Not only had we survived, but we were okay.

One of the guys with us suggested that we should do it again. Against all logic everyone, including myself, agreed. We began to climb back up to the top of the mountain. Suddenly, we were at the top. One of the guys I was with happened to be a friend of mine in real life whom we'll call Al. I didn't remember him being with me the first time we jumped off the mountain so it was interesting. I talked with him briefly. I then noticed that the mountain had changed. We were now on a balcony of some kind of multi-level apartment building. This apartment building seemed to be built right into the side of a mountain. We were on the top balcony but there were several balconies below us, like you would expect to see in an apartment building. All of the balconies were surrounded by handrails.

Al decided he was going to jump first and did a head-first dive off of the balcony we were standing on. The height was much smaller than the place we had jumped from at the outset of dream. When he jumped, there were no ledges to slap on during his downward plunge. At the last minute he tucked his legs to his chest and landed bottom-first. What looked like solid ground from the top balcony was actually very dirty water with all kinds of growth coming out of it, like a marsh. It didn't seem very deep, but the water was deep enough to break his fall. As he splashed in, a bunch of fish that were either resting or in hibernation suddenly came to the surface.

These were not typical fish. Their color was whitish-tan and their appearance was bizarre and disgusting. They actually looked like two fish melded together, the top of one being attached to the bottom of the other. In the way there are Siamese twins, these looked like Siamese fish.

Al's head emerged above the water and I knew he was fine. However, I suddenly felt really concerned. All at once the fish became aware of Al's presence and "came alive." It then became apparent that these were not two fish that were fused, but one creature whose center pivoted up. The top of what looked like one fish was actually an arm and the bottom of what looked like a second fish was the other arm. I know my description of these things may be somewhat difficult to imagine, but their appearance is not particularly important, so please bear with me.

These creatures surrounded Al, causing confusion. They began attacking him, pushing him deeper into the disgusting water and away from a place that he could get out. I began yelling at him to get out of the water but it was to no avail. At some point the other two jumped off the balcony, but I did not see them jump. All I know is that I was the only one left on the balcony.

I watched as Al was moved into the center of this marsh. As he moved deeper, other monsters came out of the water and also began to attack him. One in particular looked like a purple squid with only two legs instead of eight. The appearance was so disgusting it made my stomach turn. I considered jumping in, but I figured that if I jumped down there I would have to deal with the pain and discomfort of falling to the bottom. Furthermore, I figured I would be too busy getting attacked myself to truly help Al.

I will also note that the marsh began to look like a suburban backyard at this time. There was a fence on the back end of it that extended around the sides. It created a barrier to prevent escape. In other words, the only way for Al to get out was to get to the foot of the mountain he had jumped from. This would require him to fight his way through these appalling water creatures. At that moment I decided to pray for Al and I began to command the sea creatures that were attacking him to be bound in the name of Jesus.

Suddenly I was talking with Al and he was safe. We were standing on what appeared to be a lawn that one would find in front of a house. He had a couple scratches on his face, but other than that he was fine. I clearly remember that the scratches were not bleeding. He was out of breath and asking why I hadn't come to help him. I explained to him that I had prayed for him and that's why he was safe now. He acknowledged that he understood.

I also noticed that I had somehow gotten wet and that I was wearing swim trunks. I couldn't recall how that happened, since I'd never jumped in the water. At that moment, in the left leg part of the swim trunks, I felt like there was something that shouldn't be there. I began to squeeze the trunks from the outside and forced out a small fish. This fish began flopping up the driveway as if trying to bite something. I avoided it easily.

This creature/fish came back the other way and I avoided it again. Then I felt like there was still some other kind of sea creature in my swim trunk leg. I thought it was some kind of squid-like creature so I began to squeeze the trunks from the outside again. I squeezed it out, but before I could see what I had squeezed out I woke up. I prayed for myself and my friend.

INTERPRETING THE DREAM

When I talked to my friend about the dream, he admitted that he had been under attack. He had begun to feel very overwhelmed in his daily life. He admitted that it felt like he was somehow drowning. Furthermore, he had fallen into pornography for a short time but hadn't told anyone. In my own life, while I hadn't looked at pornography for several years by that point, I had been experiencing an unexplainable urge to give in to this sin. Nonetheless, I had been actively resisting. That's when I realized that both of us had been under attack. The difference was that I hadn't given in, so my battle wasn't as difficult.

It is clear that the water creatures in this dream represented demonic activity. Their activity seemed to be distinguished by urges towards sexual depravity and feelings of drowning, or being totally overwhelmed. The fact that I knew to pray against the water creatures and bind them in the name of Jesus clearly reveals their true identity. In the dream, both of us were afflicted by them, yet we were both delivered in relatively good shape. The question is: why should we understand these as "water spirits"? Why shouldn't we just chalk this dream up to a revelation about the external attack of an enemy that was attempting to introduce sin and bondage into our lives (fish representing run-of-the-mill demons)?

Dead in the Sea

It is difficult to give you a good answer to this question without giving a biblical premise for the issue of water spirits. So, what is the biblical premise? This next Scripture I will present to you comes from the Book of Revelation. This verse explains that at the great white throne judgment, the sea will give up the dead that are contained by it. Plainly stated, if there were no spirits in the sea, the Bible wouldn't say that there are.

"And the **sea gave up the dead which were in it**; and death and hell delivered up the dead which were in them: and they were judged every man according to their works" (Revelation 20:13).

The Bible is clear that the sea is a location of the dead just as much as hell is a location of the dead. Although this isn't commonly brought up, it doesn't make the Scripture any less relevant. As a matter of fact, Job 26:4–6 echoes this concept. This raises a valid yet extremely difficult question.

Plainly stated, are we supposed to believe that some human spirits are sent to places under water when they die as opposed to hell? If so, why didn't Jesus also mention the sea when he spoke about hell? These are difficult question indeed.

The fact of the matter is that the sea may very well serve as a holding place for spirits of dead humans. If it does, I imagine it would serve as an extension of hell. This seems to be plainly explained during the prayer of Jonah, who said, "I cried by reason of mine affliction unto the Lord, and he heard me; out of the belly of hell cried I, and thou heardest my voice. For thou hadst cast me into the deep, in the midst of the seas; and the floods compassed me about: all thy billows and thy waves passed over me" (Jonah 2:2–3). Jonah prayed this prayer from an underwater location while he was in the belly of a fish.

Taking this a step further, we have clearly resolved in former chapters that humans aren't the only kinds of creatures that die. The nephilim die and hybrids die. When they die, their spirits are not dealt with in the same way that human spirits are dealt with. Their dead spirits must go somewhere, too. Thus, they get subjugated to the spirit realm, and in this subjugation, it would only make sense that they would be assigned a location of duty from where they take their marching orders. Therefore, I propose that at least some would be assigned to take their marching orders from the sea.

THE GADARENE DEMONIAC

The Bible makes no effort to hide evidence that wickedness occurs under the sea. In key places, the Bible actually helps us to understand this issue. In fact, one of the most straightforward evidences provided to us by the Bible comes directly from the gospels. This is the case of the Gadarene (or Gerasene) demoniac. To preface this discussion, we will be focusing on the accounts in the Books of Mark and Luke. The account in the Book of

Matthew (chapter 8) mentions two demoniacs while the accounts in the books of Mark and Luke focus in on one of these two men.

When Jesus encountered a demonized man in the country of the Gadarenes, the spirits possessing the man introduced themselves as "Legion, for we are many" (Mark 5:9). They immediately began pleading with Jesus to send them into the swine as opposed to *the deep*. The story is very dramatic and has captivated readers for centuries. It has often been used as infallible evidence of the fact that demons exist. However, allow me to ask a pointed question that most have never pondered. The question is: Did the Legion actually want to be in the swine? I am firmly persuaded that the answer is no. How do I know this? Upon entering the swine they immediately drove the herd into the water, drowning the pigs. If they actually wanted to be in the swine they would have kept the pigs alive. This issue becomes the crux of the passage for our discussion.

> And they arrived at the country of the Gadarenes, which is over against Galilee. And when he went forth to land, there met him out of the city a certain man, which had devils long time, and ware no clothes, neither abode in any house, but in the tombs. When he saw Jesus, he cried out, and fell down before him, and with a loud voice said, What have I to do with thee, Jesus, thou Son of God most high? I beseech thee, torment me not. (For he had commanded the unclean spirit to come out of the man. For oftentimes it had caught him: and he was kept bound with chains and in fetters; and he brake the bands, and was driven of the devil into the wilderness.) And Jesus asked him, saying, What is thy name? And he said, Legion: because many devils were entered into him. And they besought him that he would not command them to go out into the deep. And there was there an herd of many swine feeding on the mountain: and they besought him that he would

suffer them to enter into them. And he suffered them. Then went the devils out of the man, and entered into the swine: and the herd ran violently down a steep place into the lake, and were choked.

(Luke 8:26-33)

Two things are immediately clear. The spirits did not want Jesus to send them to the deep, and the spirits went straight to the water when they got the opportunity. The word translated as *the deep* in this verse comes from the Greek word *abussos* meaning "abyss" or "bottomless pit." Whatever they would have faced there was dramatically unappealing to the spirits. Instead of taking the risk of being sent there they pled with Jesus, and with his permission, the Legion escaped to the sea. Not only did they go to the sea, but the spirits actually brought a blood sacrifice with them. In drowning the pigs, the spirits actually created a blood sacrifice as they entered the sea.

I believe that the spirits went to the sea because *that was their base of operations.* They were on assignment while they possessed the man in the country of the Gadarenes, but their assignment was interrupted by Jesus. It seems pretty clear from the account that being sent to the abyss at this time would not have been good for the Legion. Chances are that punishment and torment awaited them in the abyss for failing their assignment. Does the Bible straightforwardly state that demons get punished for incomplete assignments? No, but when the Legion pleads with Jesus to not torment them, *it becomes clear that demons can in fact be tormented.* On this note, consider the following quote from one woman who claimed to be involved in the deep occult. It speaks to the reality of how demons can actually be punished:

"Fear is a tactic that is used more often than anything else. Fear of death, fear of having your family tortured in front of your eyes. Both humans and demons were tortured. Many times demons were forced to physically manifest, then they were tortured and torn into pieces by other stronger demons because of some minor disobedience. The sights and sounds of these hideous episodes were burned into the minds of everyone present."[35]

It was once explained to me that if demons fail enough consecutive assignments, they will be sent to the abyss for punishment. We must remember that demons are not synonymous with fallen angels; they are less powerful, lower ranking, and always have to report to superiors in order to get their assignments. I believe that in light of this, they begged to be sent into the swine so they could drown the swine. By turning the herd into a blood sacrifice they were able to return to their base of operation, which was the sea by the Gadarene country. Moreover, the blood sacrifice would have permitted them to avoid punishment, since the ruling spirit that they were subject to would have been appeased by the sacrifice.

Interestingly enough, the Gadarene country as it existed in Jesus' day was completely destroyed some years after the resurrection of Jesus. The site of this city is marked by the ruins of Mukes, among which are found remains of theaters and a temple.[36] As I looked further into this issue, I realized that the temple was actually built for Zeus.[37] Note that the Roman name for the Greek God Zeus was Jupiter. It was the inscription for Jupiter that was found on the pillars of the remains at this site.[38] The spirit that was behind the idol of Zeus/Jupiter would have been the ruling spirit in the area. Furthermore, this spirit required sacrifices. Similar to the way that Jehovah required a sacrificial lamb without spot or blemish, Zeus required the sacrifice of a pig or swine. In fact, chances are that the herd was being raised for this very purpose. The Legion, knowing the preferred sacrifice of their ruling spirit, gave him the sacrifice he wanted.

To conclude our investigation into the Gadarene demoniac, I believe that if nothing else, it is obvious that the demons wanted to go to the sea.

This was their base of operations. It was in the sea that they were stationed. It was from the sea that they took their assignments. It was from the sea that the enemy exerted a heavy influence on the country of Gadara. The influence was so strong that it prevented the people from receiving anything further from God. It actually explains the conclusion of this story, which has befuddled countless Christians. When the locals found out about what Jesus had done they asked him to leave, as opposed to celebrating his power! Why would they do this? The fact of the matter is that the control and spiritual oppression from the wickedness stationed in the nearby sea prevented them from receiving Jesus.

"Then the whole multitude of the country of the Gadarenes round about besought him to depart from them; for they were taken with great fear: and he went up into the ship, and returned back again" (Luke 8:37).

LEVIATHAN

When I first began to grasp this concept, it brought a lot of clarity to me regarding this account. It is my prayer that you are finding greater clarity in light of this information as well. In any case, this isn't the only place in the Bible that references water spirits. We are now going to disclose two of the most powerful water spirits, as revealed by Scripture. Our next text comes from the Book of Psalms.

"So is this great and wide sea, wherein are things creeping innumerable, both small and great beasts. There go the ships: there is that leviathan, whom thou hast made to play therein" (Psalm 104:25-26).

Leviathan, also described in Job 41, dwells in the sea. The Book of Psalms indicates that God has made the Leviathan to "play" in the sea. It is said of Leviathan that he beholds every high thing (Job 41:34). It also says that he is king over all the children of pride. This speaks to the creature's spiritual role in the kingdom of darkness. Clearly, this is an example of underwater wickedness. While the Leviathan may have existed at that time in a physical form, the description of him goes far beyond a typical animal. In other words, Leviathan is a water spirit by nature. His description is most likely both physical and spiritual at the same time.

RAHAB

Another water spirit that is directly referenced by the Bible is the dragon Rahab. There are two Rahabs mentioned in the Bible. The Rahab that most people are familiar with is the prostitute from Jericho. She is credited with hiding the Hebrew spies before the nation of Israel conquered Jericho and began their campaign to take the Promised Land. She is mentioned in the Book of Joshua, again in the Book of Hebrews as part of the "Hall of Faith," and once more in the Book of James. The second Rahab mentioned in the Bible is what some refer to as a "mythical" sea monster (including Strong's Concordance). According to the following Psalm, God actually battled this sea monster, wounding it.

"Awake, awake, put on strength, O arm of the Lord; awake, as in the ancient days, in the generations of old. Art thou not it that hath cut Rahab, and wounded the dragon?" (Isaiah 51:9).

The Lord is credited with wounding Rahab the dragon according to this passage. In other words, God punished Rahab. The Hebrew name Rahab, according to one source, is the emblematic name of Egypt, and is also associated with the sea.[39] Although it is associated with Egypt, its origins predate the great flood of Noah's day. According to this passage, it is clear that the encounter between God and Rahab occurred in *the ancient days*—a reference to the days prior to the flood of Noah. Further revelation is provided by the Bible, which details that the wound Rahab received from God was much more than just a broken arm or a couple of stitches. God broke Rahab in pieces, a feat that would have literally destroyed the physical body of this creature.

"O Lord God of hosts, who is a strong Lord like unto thee? or to thy faithfulness round about thee? **Thou rulest the raging of the sea**: when the waves thereof arise, thou stillest them. **Thou hast broken Rahab in pieces**, as one that is slain; thou hast scattered thine enemies with thy strong arm" (Psalm 89:8-10).

This entity, crushed by God's might, continued to influence this world (particularly Egypt) as a water spirit. As to the mechanics of how all this occurred I am not entirely sure. It has been concluded by some that Rahab was and is a fallen angel.[40] I believe that it also could been the spawn of a fallen angel that had the form of a dragon—making its nature after that of the nephilim. In either case, I hypothesize that this entity manifested itself as a sea monster in the pre-flood world. After being crushed by God in that form it continued to exert its power and influence as a spirit. This spirit was probably the ruling prince over the nation of ancient Egypt from a location in the Red Sea. When God delivered the nation of Israel and caused them to cross the Red Sea on dry ground, he was reminding this spirit about who had the real power—him. Interestingly enough, the Bible even says that the strength of Egypt was Rahab! In the following verse, the word translated as *strength* is the Hebrew word *Rahab*.

"For the Egyptians shall help in vain, and to no purpose: therefore have I cried concerning this, their strength [Rahab] is to sit still" (Isaiah 30:7).

Interestingly enough, there is an ancient text known as the *Testament of Solomon*. The manuscript from which we have an English translation does not date to Solomon's day, but rather to a time after Christ's death. Nonetheless, it has some interesting things to say. I include some elements of the text here simply to provide some peripheral evidence of water spirits in non-biblical literature. Please keep in mind that I am in no way endorsing this book as infallible truth, and am fully aware that many of its claims may be false.

As the text progresses, it tells us that Solomon was able to have dominion and control over all manner of evil spirits by way of a special ring given to him by God (paired with his wisdom). He used the ring not only to summon and question demons, but also to employ them and their supernatural abilities so that the construction of the temple could be expedited. In the process he is met by quite a motley crew of characters (as one would expect).

In the midst of the text, one of the spirits that presents itself to Solomon is in the form of a horse with the behind of a fish. He explains to Solomon that he turns into waves to crash into ships, sink them, and take the riches of men. He also talks about how he makes men at sea nauseous. He concludes his response to Solomon by saying, "Behold now, in two or three days the spirit that converseth with thee will fail, because I shall have no water."[41]

This isn't the only water spirit mentioned in the text. The final spirit that Solomon meets as recorded by this book is associate with the Red Sea. Notice the references to Egypt and the situations surrounding the exodus of Israel. Could this be the same spirit named by the Bible as Rahab?

And I Solomon questioned the other spirit which came up with the pillar from the depth of the Red Sea. And I said to him: "Who art thou, and what calls thee? And what is thy business? For I hear many things about thee." And the demon answered: "I, O King Solomon, am called Abezithibod. I am a descendant of the archangel. Once as I sat in the first heaven, of which the name is Ameleouth -- I then am a fierce spirit and winged, and with a single wing, plotting against every spirit under heaven. I was present when Moses went in before Pharaoh, king of Egypt, and I hardened his heart. I am he whom Iannes and Iambres invoked homing with Moses in Egypt. I am he who fought against Moses with wonders with signs."

I said therefore to him: "How wast thou found in the Red Sea?" And he answered: "In the exodus of the sons of Israel I hardened the heart of Pharaoh. And I excited his heart and that of his ministers. And I caused them to pursue after the children of Israel. And Pharaoh followed with (me) and all the Egyptians. Then I was present there, and we followed together. And we all came up upon the Red Sea. And it came to pass when the children of Israel had crossed over, the water returned and hid all the host of the Egyptians and all their might. And I remained in the sea, being kept under this pillar. But when Ephippas came, being sent by thee, shut up in the vessel of a flask, he fetched me up to thee."[42]

There is no question that exploration in extra-biblical texts can yield some radically fascinating insights that may or may not be entirely true. However, according to the Bible, both Rahab and Leviathan represent sea spirits. Furthermore, the evidence clearly points to the existence of water spirits in the case of the Gadarene demoniac. To ignore the plain revelation of Scripture on the issue of water spirits is, in my opinion, an act of willful ignorance. This chapter was written with the purpose of explaining why God had stored up an army of water spirits (angels) in my heavenly mansion to go into the waters of the earth and destroy the works of darkness in those places. Paired with the anecdotal story I shared earlier regarding the dimensional raid on the underwater prison, there is a powerful witness to these things. Why would I waste his provision to get things done simply because I don't want to believe? Furthermore, why would you?

CHAPTER 18

An Introduction to Portals

A portal is defined as a door, gate, or entrance, especially one of imposing appearance, as to a palace.[43] For our purposes, the word *portal* will be used to explain the phenomena of opening doorways or gateways between different dimensions and across space-time. For this reason, they can also be understood as wormholes, which are defined by the dictionary as tunnels in the geometry of space-time postulated to connect different parts of the universe.[44] Space-time is simply the four-dimensional continuum, having three spatial coordinates (length, width, and height) and one temporal coordinate (time), in which all physical quantities may be located.[45] In light of this, our definition of wormholes will extend slightly beyond the definition stated by the dictionary (limiting the activity of wormholes to the confines of our universe) because we will soon see that portals are also used for travel between the second and third heavens (meaning between dimensions higher than the fourth dimension).

Portals are absolutely central to the workings of the spirit realm. Traversing dimensions and ultimately accessing the kingdom of God requires the use of portals. Unfortunately, because teaching on this topic is virtually non-existent, our understanding of what portals might be has been skewed. When we hear the word *portal*, most of us immediately think of something one might find in a science fiction movie. We may think of a giant engraved circle like in the movie *Star Gate*. Once activated, this circle opens a veritable wormhole capable of transferring individuals to different worlds, universes, and realities. Alternatively, we may think of a UFO conspiracy theory. In the end, few of us will associate the word *portal* with anything of biblical significance.

While I'm not going to tell you that the ideas suggested by science fiction are impossible, I am going to state at the outset of this chapter that I am not going to rely on the conjectures of science fiction to communicate the relevance of portals. Instead, I am going to primarily rely on the truth of the word of God. What I have found is that the Bible is chock full of references to portals. The Bible even references different types of portals!

THE TOWER OF BABEL

I believe that the first clear attempt by men to use a portal (or to open a wormhole) was recorded in the Book of Genesis shortly after the flood had destroyed the "old world." The incident was known as the Tower of Babel. I use the word *attempt* in reference to the Tower of Babel effort because those involved didn't actually succeed in completing it. Before they were able to achieve their goals, God put a stop to the entire effort by confusing the languages of the world. This story begins only a few generations after the great flood.

In those days, a man by the name of Nimrod began to become very powerful in the earth (Genesis 10:8-10). Nimrod was the son of Cush, who was the son of Ham, who in turn was the son of Noah. This means that Nimrod was Noah's great-grandchild. Furthermore, based on Noah's age at his death (950 years old), they were actually alive at the same time. The Bible is clear that at this time the whole earth was of one language and one speech.

"And the whole earth was of one language and of one accent *and* mode of expression" (Genesis 11:1 AMPC).

As we read the account of Nimrod, we learn that the beginning of his kingdom was Babel (Genesis 10:10). This means that he was in power when the agenda to build the Tower of Babel came into consideration. What was the purpose of the Tower of Babel? According to the Bible, they wanted to make a tower whose top would reach to heaven. What could this have meant?

"And it came to pass, as they journeyed from the east, that they found a plain in the land of Shinar; and they dwelt there. And they said one to another, Go to, let us make brick, and burn them thoroughly. And they had brick for stone, and slime had they for morter. And they said, Go to, let us build us a city and a tower, whose top may reach unto heaven; and let us make us a name, lest we be scattered abroad upon the face of the whole earth" (Genesis 11:2-4).

Many people, ignorant of just how advanced and intelligent these people were, have assumed that the Tower of Babel was simply intended to be a tall monument that would cause the builders to be remembered for generations. This thought requires the assumption that their definition of heaven was simply the sky. The issue is that if we really think about it, this notion is ridiculous. The reason it is ridiculous is *because of the <u>concern</u>* that God had regarding this agenda. If it was simply intended to be a tall building, I doubt God would have responded in the way he did. This is what Scripture reveals:

And the Lord came down to see the city and the tower, which the children of men builded. **And the Lord said, Behold, the people is one, and they have all one language; and this they begin to do: and now nothing will be restrained from them, which they have imagined to do. Go to, let us go down, and there confound their language, that they may not understand one another's speech**. So the Lord scattered them abroad from thence upon the face of all the earth: and they left off to build the city. Therefore is the name of it called Babel; because the Lord did there confound the language of all the earth: and from thence did the Lord scatter them abroad upon the face of all the earth.

(Genesis 11:5-9)

In response to this project, God declared that the people were *one*, and if they would have succeeded in their agenda to build the tower, *nothing* would have been restrained from them. The weight of this comment is so fantastic it is almost impossible to accept. This comment reveals the astronomical power of unity amongst men. Whether the agenda is of God or not, the power that united humanity taps into is virtually incomprehensible. This is why the devil works so hard to unite people around his agendas, and likewise why God wants Christians to be united as *one* (John 17:21-23).

Before going further, I want to interject that when God said "the people is one" he wasn't actually referring to every person alive, as some have falsely concluded. The Bible says that the whole earth had one language, but it never says that they all, without exception, submitted to Nimrod and his kingdom. When God said that "the people is one" he was referring to everyone who had joined themselves to Nimrod and his kingdom. This would have understandably excluded Noah and any others following Noah's example. Melchizedek, the priest of the Most High God, would have also been excluded, as well as Abraham. Many are surprised to learn that they were all alive at the same time.

Having said this, the question is properly asked: how could a building that was merely intended to be tall have this kind of impact? The answer is that the tower of Babel was never intended to be just a tall building. The key phrase is that they wanted to build the tower *to heaven*. In other words, they wanted to build a tower that would function as a gateway to higher dimensions. This is what concerned God—not the mere capability of the building to achieve a certain height.

Further insight into this issue can be extracted from a historical text known as the *Book of Jasher*. While I do not endorse the *Book of Jasher* as an infallible text, I do believe that, like any other historical document, it contains at least some information that is true. I also believe that much of what it says where the Bible is silent helps to bring clarity to the biblical text. Like the *Book of 1 Enoch*, the *Book of Jasher* in its original manuscript is actually endorsed by the Bible. It is referenced by name in both Joshua 10:13 and 2 Samuel 1:18. The question is not whether the Bible endorses the text, but whether or not the *Book of Jasher* that we have today is true to the original manuscript. Since the Spirit of God did not see fit to canonize this book we are limited to referencing it as a historical document. While I would advise anyone to take what this book says with a grain of salt, I believe that what it has to say on the issue of Babel is worth repeating. The text clearly indicates the true agenda behind the building of Babel.

> And all the princes of Nimrod and his great men took counsel together; Phut, Mitzraim, Cush and Canaan with their families, and they said to each other, Come let us build ourselves a city and in it a strong tower, and its top reaching heaven, and we will make ourselves famed, so that we may reign upon the

whole world, in order that the evil of our enemies may cease from us, that we may reign mightily over them, and that we may not become scattered over the earth on account of their wars. And they all went before the king, and they told the king these words, and the king agreed with them in this affair, and he did so. And all the families assembled consisting of about six hundred thousand men, and they went to seek an extensive piece of ground to build the city and the tower, and they sought in the whole earth and they found none like one valley at the east of the land of Shinar, about two days' walk, and they journeyed there and they dwelt there. And they began to make bricks and burn fires to build the city and the tower that they had imagined to complete. **And the building of the tower was unto them a transgression and a sin, and they began to build it, and whilst they were building against the Lord God of heaven, they imagined in their hearts to war against him and to ascend into heaven.** And all these people and all the families divided themselves in three parts; the first said We will ascend into heaven and fight against him; the second said, We will ascend to heaven and place our own gods there and serve them; and the third part said, We will ascend to heaven and smite him with bows and spears; and God knew all their works and all their evil thoughts, and he saw the city and the tower which they were building.

(Jasher 9:21–26)[46]

While the building was described as being a very tall structure, the purpose was not simply to be tall. It was to provide a method by which men could ascend to heaven. In order to make war with God these men would have had to cross dimensions, and from God's response in Genesis, it appears that without direct intervention, they would have succeeded. How would they have used the tower to cross dimensions? Somehow, the tower would have been designed to function as a gateway to a higher dimension. Thus, it would have been designed to open a portal (or wormhole) for that purpose.

While this may seem slightly far-fetched, it is widely known that the ziggurats that exist throughout the world were built with this purpose in mind. A ziggurat is a temple of Sumerian origin in the form of a pyramidal tower, consisting of a number of stories and having about the outside a broad ascent winding round the structure, presenting the appearance of a series of terraces.[47] Ziggurats are more commonly referred to as step pyramids. According to one source, "high" temples, such as the ziggurats, were not intended for public worship or ceremonies, but were instead used as "a portal by a god on his visits to the earth."[48] In other words, fallen angels used ziggurats in order to cross out of their respective dimensions and into ours. If this was the clear purpose of these structures, why would we conclude anything less of the Tower of Babel, whose purpose was clearly spelled out?

THE HORROR OF GREAT DARKNESS

The next type of portal that we will discuss answers a lot of theological questions. It helps us to make sense of several difficult passages of Scripture. Our discussion begins with an encounter that Abraham had with the Most High God. The account begins as the word of the Lord appears to Abraham in a vision.

"After these things the word of the Lord came unto Abram in a vision, saying, Fear not, Abram: I am thy shield, and thy exceeding great reward" (Genesis 15:1).

When this happened, Abraham (still being called Abram) responded to God with his concerns. He still did not have an heir and he was getting old. While he desperately wanted to continue believing God, the circumstantial evidence was not in his favor. For this reason he was concerned that someone born in his house by the name of Eliezar would have no choice but to stand in as his heir, since he yet remained childless. In response to his concern God reaffirmed his promise that one born of his own bowels would be his heir.

"And Abram said, Lord God, what wilt thou give me, seeing I go childless, and the steward of my house is this Eliezer of Damascus? And Abram said, Behold, to me thou hast given no seed: and, lo, one born in my house is mine heir. And, behold, the word of the Lord came unto him, saying, This shall not be thine heir; but he that shall come forth out of thine own bowels shall be thine heir" (Genesis 15:2–4).

God then proceeded to show Abraham the stars of the sky. He told Abraham that his seed would number as the stars of the heaven. As God watched Abraham's response he was pleased. This is because Abraham believed him, in spite of all the circumstantial evidence. For this reason the Bible says that his act of believing God was accounted to him for righteousness (Galatians 3:6). In other words, the fact that he chose to believe God placed him in right standing with God.

The Lord continued to speak to Abraham, declaring that he had given to him and his seed the Promised Land. In response, Abraham posed to God a question. He wanted evidence. He asked God to give him something by which he would know that he was truly assigned to inherit the land. God responded with some specific directions for Abraham to follow. The instructions involved the preparation of animal sacrifices that would be used for the creation of a covenant between God and Abraham. What Abraham didn't know was that God planned to make this covenant of his own accord, ultimately cutting a covenant with himself that would not make any future requirements of Abraham.

The preparation required Abraham to kill five animals and arrange their carcasses in a specific manner. He was to take a three-year-old heifer, a three-year-old she goat, a three-year-old ram, a turtle dove and a young pigeon. After killing them he was to cut their carcasses in half (except for the birds) and lay them side by side. The purpose was to create a path between the pieces of flesh. When this path was walked, the result would be the ratification of a covenant (Genesis 15:8–10).

To *covenant* means "to cut." In essence, covenants were not typically established without the shedding of blood. This is the difference between a covenant and a contract. A covenant exists in the spirit as a living pact between parties. The life of any covenant is generated by the blood that was shed in its creation. Thus, the most powerful covenant ever created involved Jesus Christ shedding the very blood of God in order to create the New Covenant. Nonetheless, here we find Abraham shedding the blood of the prescribed animals in order to cut a covenant between him and God.

After the sacrificial animals had been arranged according to God's instructions, Abraham waited for God to show up. Over time birds tried to peck at the carcasses but Abraham drove them away. However, like any normal person, Abraham began to get tired. Eventually a deep sleep fell upon him, which probably had just as much to do with God as it had to do with Abraham's physical exhaustion. When Abraham had fallen asleep one of the most bizarre verses in the Bible is recorded. It reads as follows:

"And when the sun was going down, a deep sleep fell upon Abram; and, lo, an horror of great darkness fell upon him" (Genesis 15:12).

When we think about God, we often associate him with light. This should come as no surprise, since the Bible straightforwardly states that God is Light (1 John 1:5). We associate him with glory, with peace, with joy, and with majesty. However, in this verse we find that a horror of great darkness falls upon Abraham. It wouldn't be so confounding if not for the fact that the very next verse records the speech of God (not the devil like we might expect when we read about the horror of great darkness).

This puzzled me for a long time until God opened my eyes to portals. That's when I was able to understand that the horror of great darkness wasn't due to God's presence. It was actually the result of the portal that God had opened up in order to step into Abraham's time-space and participate in the covenant-making process. What was it about the opening of a portal that caused the horror of great darkness? This would have been the result of violent clouds that formed around the portal as part of the earth's natural response to the type of wormhole required for God to travel between the first and third heavens. We see this same phenomenon occur in the Book of Ezekiel.

THE THRONE OF GOD

And I looked, and, behold, a whirlwind came out of the north, a great cloud, and a fire infolding itself, and a brightness was about it, and out of the midst thereof as the colour of amber, out of the midst of the fire. Also out of the midst thereof came the likeness of four living creatures. And this was their appearance; they had the likeness of a man. And every one had four faces, and every one had four wings... And above the firmament that was over their heads was the likeness of a throne, as the appearance of a sapphire stone: and upon the likeness of the throne was the likeness as the appearance of a man above upon it. And I saw as the colour of amber, as the appearance of fire round about within it, from the appearance of his loins even upward, and from the appearance of his loins even downward, I saw as it were the appearance of fire, and it had brightness round about. As the appearance of the bow that is in the cloud in the day of rain, so was the appearance of the brightness round about. This was the appearance of the likeness of the glory of the Lord. And when I saw it, I fell upon my face, and I heard a voice of one that spake.

(Ezekiel 1:4–6, 26–28)

As a young Christian, the Book of Ezekiel (particularly the first chapter) was so far over my head I just kind of skipped right over it. I have since learned that this issue was not exclusive to me. The problem is that what we see being described here is far beyond the average Christian's frame of reference. Frankly, most of us have had no basis out of which to comprehend this passage. Without leaders in our lives to straightforwardly tell us what to believe about this passage, it remains an illusory non-essential for many people. This was true for me until the day came that God decided to change this fact in my life.

I distinctly remember that during my second year of Bible school, I began to voraciously read and meditate on this chapter. It became like an obsession. Over and over again I would read the words of Ezekiel and over and over again I said to myself, "I just don't get it. What am I missing?" For some reason, unlike before, I couldn't just let it go. I began to ask others what their perspectives were. I regularly engaged people in conversation about this passage as I fervently searched for answers. My thoughts would drift to this passage daily, and I knew that until I learned what God wanted me to know, this fact wasn't going to change.

Then one day it clicked. The resulting revelation was extraordinary to me. *I realized that I was reading about the entrance of God's throne into Ezekiel's time-space.* The throne of God has wheels (Ezekiel 1:16, Daniel 7:9–10) and is carried by entities referred to as living creatures. When Ezekiel described the "whirlwind out of the North, a great cloud, and a fire enfolding itself" he was talking about the earth's response to the portal that had just opened. The opening of this particular type of wormhole results in a great and dark cloud manifesting around it.

This great cloud enfolding itself was the same horror of darkness that Abraham experienced when God cut the covenant with him. It wasn't God that was a horror of darkness, it was the portal that opened to allow God a literal entrance into our dimension. In Ezekiel's account, God enters upon his throne accompanied by four living creatures. The fact that God has entered the scene and is seated upon his throne is inarguable once we understand what we're reading. In the subsequent chapters, God addresses the prophet on a large number of subjects. The one seated upon the throne who had just entered through the portal is God, and the one that addresses the prophet in the subsequent chapters is God. Consider the first four verses of the very next chapter in the Book of Ezekiel.

"And He said to me [Ezekiel], Son of man, stand upon your feet and I will speak to you. And the Spirit entered into me when He spoke to me and set me upon my feet, and I heard Him speaking to me. And He said to me, I send you, son of man, to the children of Israel, two rebellious nations that have rebelled against Me. They and their fathers have transgressed against Me even to this very day. And the children are impudent and hard of heart. **I send you to them and you shall say to them, Thus, says the Lord God**" (Ezekiel 2:1–4 AMPC).

PORTALS IN THE HEAVENS

Thus far we have established that certain types of structures placed in key locations (like the Tower of Babel built in Shinar) can be used to open portals. We have also established that God can open portals from the third heaven and into our realm. Specific to the Tower of Babel incident, the goal was to build a portal in order to access the third heaven. While we must accept that first heaven to third heaven portals can theoretically be opened by man, we must also acknowledge that at least on that occasion, God stopped it. Conversely, in the case of ziggurats, the purpose of these structures seemed to be primarily for the purpose of generating portals between the first and second heavens. Thus, the "gods," or fallen angels, would use them to make their entrance from where they are and into our time-space.

We have also learned that God uses portals in order to manifest himself into the earth. The portals that we see going between the third heaven and the first heaven in Scripture are generated by God. When these portals occur they are accompanied by dark clouds, fire enfolding itself, and other extraordinary visual manifestations. This same phenomenon accompanied God's appearance to Moses at Sinai. When God showed up the same thick, dark clouds were present, again signifying the open portal that had manifested.

"And the Lord said unto Moses, Lo, I come unto thee in a **thick cloud**, that the people may hear when I speak with thee, and believe thee for ever. And Moses told the words of the people unto the Lord" (Exodus 19:9).

Electricity and Portals

On this note we find another phenomenon related to portal activity that warrants mentioning. It appears as though electrical activity can be associated with portals. When God appeared on Mount Sinai, we find the following description of the event.

"And it came to pass on the third day in the morning, that there were thunders and **lightnings**, and a thick cloud upon the mount, and the voice of the trumpet exceeding loud; so that all the people that was in the camp trembled" (Exodus 19:16).

Lightning is nothing more than an electrical discharge. It is electricity. In Exodus 19, Jehovah had opened a portal in order to introduce himself to the recently delivered nation of Israel. During this event, we find that lightning was upon the mountain in addition to the thick cloud. While it is true that both lightning (Revelation 4:5) and fire (Daniel 7:10) proceed forth from the throne of God, it seems that electricity is also tied to portal activity.

This is interesting because, when observing certain cases of demonic activity, I have found that spirits seem to be able to manipulate electrical currents. For instance, lights can be turned on and off. As a matter of fact, I even remember when I made a decision to seek God and receive the baptism of the Holy Spirit. In an attempt to dissuade me, I believe a spirit either showed up or got stirred up. I was playing worship music in my parents' house as I attempted to seek God. I was seventeen at the time. Can you believe that this spirit had to nerve to lower the volume and then turn the music off! I remember the chill that went through me when that happened. I immediately rebuked the spirit in the name of Jesus, even though I didn't see it with my physical eyes. It was maybe fifteen or twenty minutes later that I first spoke in tongues. Praise God!

"And these signs shall follow them that believe; In my name shall they cast out devils; they shall speak with new tongues" (Mark 16:17).

More to Come

Amazingly enough, this is not the end of the discussion. There are also second heaven to third heaven portals. While we don't get told as much detail about them, we easily conclude that these portals exist based on simple logic. One example, which was discussed in the beginning of this book, is revealed in the account of Jacob's ladder (Genesis 28:12). Jacob saw angels ascending and descending from the throne of God. In this case, the portal appeared similar to a ladder. These angels, however, remained in the spirit realm and did not manifest in the flesh. This means that the portal they were using went from the third heaven to the second heaven. Another example of this type of portal is indirectly referenced later on in Israel's history.

CHAPTER 19

Further Inquiry into Portals

In the Book of Daniel, the prophet committed himself to a fast in order to seek God on a matter. Twenty-one days later, a heavenly messenger arrived who immediately explained to Daniel that he was sent on the first day that Daniel committed himself to pray and to seek God.

"Then said he unto me, Fear not, Daniel: for from the first day that thou didst set thine heart to understand, and to chasten thyself before thy God, thy words were heard, and I am come for thy words. But the prince of the kingdom of Persia withstood me one and twenty days: but, lo, Michael, one of the chief princes, came to help me; and I remained there with the kings of Persia" (Daniel 10:12–13).

According to the heavenly messenger, his trip was interrupted by a confrontation with the prince of Persia. How does this story help us to understand that there are portals between the second and third heavens? We must keep in mind that God has planted his throne in the third heaven. Therefore, the third heaven is where the angels of God receive their orders. These angels go forth from that place upon receiving their orders (or assignments). Wherever they wind up going, we must understand that their trip begins in the realm of the third heaven.

That the prince of Persia was obviously not human is clear from the context of the passage. How could a mere mortal hold up a heavenly messenger for twenty-one days? This helps us understand quite a bit. It forces us to conclude that the prince of Persia was a powerful fallen angel that held authority over the region of Persia. He didn't battle with the heavenly messenger on the earth, but in the heavens (the second heaven, to be specific). This should be common knowledge for most Christians who have studied this passage.

Per our discussion, the point I want to get across is that the heavenly messenger had to use a specific mode of transportation in order to transition from the third heaven to the place in the second heaven where the conflict erupted. What was the mode of transportation? Simply put, it was a portal. Any time dimensions are either being ascended or descended, some form of a portal is being employed. I use the phrase "some form of" because I want to be clear that there are different types of portals.

The same principle is observed in the Book of Job. When Satan was brought before God, a portal would have been employed as well.

"Again there was a day when the sons of God came to present themselves before the Lord, and Satan came also among them to present himself before the Lord" (Job 2:1).

MANOAH'S ANGEL

Believe it or not, fire is actually defined by Scripture as an avenue through which a portal can be opened to the spirit realm. When we begin to grasp this concept, it takes the significance of occult practices such as "passing infants through the fire" to another level. It also helps us to understand the spiritual significance of burnt offerings in the Old Testament. In order to communicate this concept, we will discuss two stories that clearly reveal this function of fire. The first occurs in the Book of Judges and involves the parents of Samson. Samson was a judge of Israel in the days before God granted Israel the right to have kings. He ultimately delivered the nation from a lot of the persecution coming from the Philistines. This act of deliverance unfortunately cost him his life due to poor decision making on his part.

Prior to his birth, Samson's parents experienced a visitation from an angel. Just like the angels that appeared to Abraham and later delivered Lot before the destruction of Sodom and Gomorrah (Genesis 18-19), this angel appeared as a man. The story (found in Judges 13) outlines that Samson's mother was barren. One day, an angel of the Lord appeared to her and told her that she would be having a son, who was to be a Nazarite unto God from the womb. This means that the child, among other things, wasn't to cut his hair. The angel went on to explain to Samson's mother that she was to not drink any kind of alcohol, and that she was not to eat any unclean thing during the pregnancy.

As a result, Samson's mother-to-be went to her husband, Manoah, to tell him the great news. She explained to him that a "man of God" had told her that she would soon conceive. Manoah's immediate response was to pray to God so that the "man" that had prophesied to his wife would come to them again and give them further instructions. God answered this prayer, and shortly afterwards the angel, again appearing as a man, met Samson's mother in the field. She fetched her husband and brought him to the angel, who gave him the same instructions he had given her in the beginning. This was Manoah's reaction:

"And Manoah said unto the angel of the Lord, I pray thee, let us detain thee, until we shall have made ready a kid for thee. And the angel of the Lord said unto Manoah, Though thou detain me, I will not eat of thy bread: and if thou wilt offer a burnt offering, thou must offer it unto the Lord. For Manoah knew not that he was an angel of the Lord" (Judges 13:15–16).

Manoah wanted to detain and feed the one he was speaking with since he had no idea that he was actually speaking to an angel. The angel obliged Manoah by agreeing to hang around for a brief time, but made it clear that he would not be joining them for a meal. The next part of the story reveals ability for fire to be used as a portal. Manoah prepared a sacrifice to the Lord and put it in a fire to be consumed. Manoah had no idea that during this moment, the fire actually became a doorway to the spirit realm. This quickly came to light as the angel proceeded to step into the fire in its physical body. The Bible says that the angel did wondrously, and exited their time-space through the portal.

"So Manoah took a kid with a meat offering, and offered it upon a rock unto the Lord: and the angel did wonderously; and Manoah and his wife looked on. For it came to pass, when the flame went up toward heaven from off the altar, that the angel of the Lord ascended in the flame of the altar. And Manoah and his wife looked on it, and fell on their faces to the ground" (Judges 13:19–20).

This story reveals that fire has certain properties that allow it to function as a portal to the spirit realm. This is particularly true when it is being used for the purpose of offering up sacrifices. In this particular case, they witnessed an angel exiting our time-space and entering the spirit realm. Considering that a door always opens up a passage in two directions, it can also be concluded that fire can allow for spiritual being to be brought from the spiritual realm and into our world (and even manifest in a physical body). The next story clearly details this type of activity.

THE FIERY FURNACE

In the Book of Daniel there is a famous story in which three Hebrew boys named Shadrach, Meshach, and Abednego are cast into a furnace of fire because of their refusal to worship the image of gold that king Nebuchadnezzar (the king of Babylon) had made of himself. Upon learning about their refusal, Nebuchadnezzar ordered them to be burned in a furnace of fire. Not only were they to be burned, but the furnace was even heated to seven times its normal temperature to ensure their destruction! As a matter of fact, the furnace was so hot that the soldiers that threw these Hebrews into the fire died in the process. In the midst of this impossible situation, a miracle took place.

"And these three men, Shadrach, Meshach, and Abednego, fell down bound into the burning fiery furnace. Then Nebuchadnezzar the king [saw and] was astounded, and he jumped up and said to his counselors, Did we not cast three men bound into the midst of the fire? They answered, True, O king. He answered, Behold, I see four men loose, walking in the midst of the fire, and they are not hurt! And the form of the fourth is like a son of the gods!" (Daniel 3:23–25 AMPC).

Once Shadrach, Meshach, and Abednego found themselves bound in the midst of the fiery furnace, they remained unharmed. Furthermore, there was a fourth person seen walking among them. This was a heavenly being, quite possibly a theophany (meaning an appearance of Jesus Christ in the Old Testament). How did the fourth person enter the scene? Through the use of a portal the heavenly being crossed over into their time-space in order to protect them and bring glory to the God of heaven. This portal opened in order to serve as a doorway from the spirit realm and into this world. Furthermore, it opened in the midst of a fire, just like the portal the angel used when departing from Samson's parents. Clearly, fire seems to have the capacity to open wormholes to the spirit realm under certain circumstances.

The Bottomless Pit

While it is incredibly exciting to come to the understanding that portals allow for God and other heavenly beings to enter into our time-space, there is another side to this issue. While I don't want to spend too much time on this point, I do want to make it clear that portals can be opened to the realms of the second heaven. Keep in mind that this is where one will find fallen spirit beings, hell, the pit, and other components of the kingdom of darkness. We will look at two examples of portals that were opened to these realms

Our first example of a portal being opened up to a location that exists in the second heaven occurs in the Book of Revelation. This passage describes an angel opening the bottomless pit in order to release a horrible plague upon the earth. Prior to opening the pit, this angel first obtains its key. How this angel gets this key and whose side the angel is on remains somewhat of a mystery. In any case, whatever this key is, it allows him to open this place onto the earth. The result is that horrific hybridized creatures are released into the earth to cause great torment.

> Then the fifth angel blew [his] trumpet, and I saw a star that had fallen from the sky to the earth; and to the angel was given the key of the shaft of the Abyss (the bottomless pit). He opened the long shaft of the Abyss (the bottomless pit), and smoke like the smoke of a huge furnace puffed out of the long shaft, so that the sun and the atmosphere were darkened by the smoke from the long shaft. Then out of the smoke locusts

came forth on the earth, and such power was granted them as the power the earth's scorpions have... The locusts resembled horses equipped for battle. On their heads was something like golden crowns. Their faces resembled the faces of people. They had hair like the hair of women, and their teeth were like lions' teeth. Their breastplates (scales) resembled breastplates made of iron, and the [whirring] noise made by their wings was like the roar of a vast number of horse-drawn chariots going at full speed into battle. They have tails like scorpions, and they have stings, and in their tails lies their ability to hurt men for [the] five months.

(Revelation 9:1–3, 7–10 AMPC).

The Witch at Endor

Our next text comes from the Book of 1 Samuel. On this occasion, King Saul had made a trip to the witch at Endor wearing a disguise. He was hoping to find some answers, and wanted to speak to the deceased prophet Samuel. Although she didn't want to cooperate at first, she was persuaded after a short discourse. When she proceeded to perform her witchcraft, she opened up a portal. Out of this portal she described a terrifying super-human entity coming up from the earth, and then identified this spirit as Samuel. Whether this was Samuel's actual spirit that was resting in para-dise (which, prior to Jesus "taking captivity captive" would have existed as an extension of Hades) or a demon masquerading as Samuel (as some have suggested) is not a question I'm going address at length. My personal opinion is that this was actually Samuel. However, the simple fact is that regardless of what we believe about the spirit that shows up, this portal clearly acted as a gateway between the first and second heavens.

So Saul disguised himself, put on other raiment, and he and two men with him went and came to the woman at night. He said to her, Perceive for me by the familiar spirit and bring up for me the dead person whom I shall name to you. The woman said, See here, you know what Saul has done, how he has cut off those who are mediums and wizards out of the land. Why then do you lay a trap for my life to cause my death? And Saul swore to her by the Lord, saying, As the Lord lives, there shall no punishment come to you for this. The woman said, Whom shall I bring up for you? He said, Bring up Samuel for me. And when the woman saw Samuel, she screamed and she said to Saul, Why have you deceived me? For you are Saul! The king said to her, Be not afraid; what do you see? The woman said to Saul, I see a god [terrifying superhuman being] coming up out of the earth! He said to her, In what form is he? And she said, An old man comes up, covered with a mantle. And Saul perceived that it was Samuel, and he stooped with his face to the ground and made obeisance.

(1 Samuel 28:8–14 AMPC)

The idea to take away from this discussion is that the enemy knows about the function and purpose of portals. He knows how to use them for his purposes and agendas. Furthermore, he can even train humans in their use as they submit themselves to him. Portals can be used as bridges between other dimensions to allow extremely evil entities to gain entrance into our world. Since a door always opens up from two ends, we can also conclude that portals can be used to extract humans into other dimensions for the devil's purposes. The most profound element of this discussion is that in light of all of this there remains nothing to fear: _because of the power of Jesus Christ_. The Bible is clear that Jesus spoiled (or triumphed over) every evil and wicked entity (whether angel or demon). Furthermore, it is his presence in and around Christians that empowers us to live according to his victory.

"And having spoiled principalities and powers, he made a shew of them openly, triumphing over them in it" (Colossians 2:15).

THE TRANSFIGURATION

I would be doing the reader a disservice by not spending a bit of time discussing one last portal. This portal occurred during an event known as the transfiguration. Before I get to the actual event, I want to present a Scripture that confounded me for several years. It confounded me because I could not figure out how there could be people who had heard what Jesus was saying and would not taste death until they "saw the kingdom of God." Taking the following passage at face value, few would realistically argue that it does not come off as confounding.

> And he said to them all, If any man will come after me, let him deny himself, and take up his cross daily, and follow me. For whosoever will save his life shall lose it: but whosoever will lose his life for my sake, the same shall save it. For what is a man advantaged, if he gain the whole world, and lose himself, or be cast away? For whosoever shall be ashamed of me and of my words, of him shall the Son of man be ashamed, when he shall come in his own glory, and in his Father's, and of the holy angels. But I tell you of a truth, **there be some standing here, which shall not taste of death, till they see the kingdom of God**.
>
> (Luke 9:23–27)

Two thousand years have passed since this event, yet God has not established his kingdom on earth in any physical sense. It only exists in the hearts of believers (Luke 17:21) and becomes revealed through their works of faith and labors of love (1 Thessalonians 1:3). How could there be some that would not taste death until they saw the kingdom of God? I have honestly pondered the idea that there may be people in the earth today that have lived since the time of Christ. What if God made them immortal in light of this verse? The problem is that realistically, this seems to make little sense. The question remains: what are we to do with this comment?

When God opened my eyes to the resolution of this mystery I was quite excited. The answer is actually revealed in the very next part of Luke chapter 9. There is really no guesswork involved. As it turns out, Jesus was referring to Peter, James, and John when he used the phrase "there be some." These men formed an inner circle with Jesus, even amongst the twelve disciples. Jesus shared an extra-special relationship with these men. They were made privy to things that not all of the other apostles were made privy to.

About eight days after Jesus made his confounding remark, these men were involved in a radical encounter. What they encountered was more than just a revelation of who Jesus was, it was an encounter with the kingdom of God itself. Moreover, it involved the same phenomena we have been looking at throughout this chapter—namely, the opening of a portal into our time-space with the presence of a cloud. In addition, there was an overlay upon our dimension by the spirits of Moses and Elijah, who were permitted to talk with Jesus on this occasion. The event went on to be known as the Transfiguration, and it involved portal activity.

And it came to pass about an eight days after these sayings, he took Peter and John and James, and went up into a mountain to pray. And as he prayed, the fashion of his countenance was altered, and his raiment was white and glistering. And, behold, there talked with him two men, which were Moses and Elias: Who appeared in glory, and spake of his decease which he should accomplish at Jerusalem. But Peter and they that were with him were heavy with sleep: and when they were awake, they saw his glory, and the two men that stood with him. And it came to pass, as they departed from him, Peter said unto Jesus, Master, it is good for us to be here: and let us make three tabernacles; one for thee, and one for Moses, and one for Elias: not knowing what he said. **While he thus, spake, there came a cloud, and overshadowed them: and they feared as they entered into the cloud**. And there came a voice out of the cloud, saying, This is my beloved Son: hear him. And when the voice was past, Jesus was found alone. And they kept it close, and told no man in those days any of those things which they had seen.

(Luke 9:28–36)

It is interesting to note that as Jesus prayed and his countenance was changed, the disciples fell asleep. When the presence of God is very strong, an overwhelming peace accompanies it that can cause people to drift right into heavy sleep. I have witnessed this happen at times when I have entered into the presence of the Lord with others around. Many who worshipfully quiet themselves before God in an attempt to hear from him will find themselves drifting right off to sleep the first time they try. His extreme presence can result in different manifestations, but at times it will put people right into a heavy sleep.

When they awoke, they witnessed Moses and Elijah speaking with Jesus. Since Moses and Elijah were not living on earth at that time, they had clearly made their entrance from another realm. As they were leaving there came a cloud, which overshadowed Jesus and the apostles. It was at this point that Peter, James, and John entered what could be described as a dimensional rift. They were caused to enter into another realm entirely, and it was frightening! Out of the cloud came the voice of the Father to declare the true identity of Jesus. Jesus was the Son of God, and his true nature was glorious! Moreover, Peter had to put his foot in his mouth once again as this gentle reminder from the Father made it clear that we need not make tabernacles to Moses and Elijah, it is Jesus we must hear. Jesus is the only Way, and no man can come to the Father except through him (John 14:6). He is our only true portal, or doorway, to God.

This takes us into the last part of this book, which deals with the temple and the glory. As incredible as it is to learn about geographic portals that are discussed by the Bible, the subject does not end with this revelation. There are both external and internal portals. Internal portals are portals that exist within humans. Comprehending this takes us into the final part of our journey, during which we will deal with the temple and the glory. The ramifications prove revolutionary.

CHAPTER 20

The Temple and the Glory

The first temple to Jehovah was completed under the rule of Solomon, who went down in the annals of history as Israel's most prosperous king. His father was the famous King David who slew giants and united the nation of Israel. David had begun making preparations for the temple's construction by securing necessary materials. However, due to the fact that he was a man of war, God would not permit him to build the temple (1 Chronicles 28:3). This responsibility fell to his son Solomon.

THE DEDICATION OF THE TEMPLE

Solomon's job was to see to its completion. During his rule, Solomon finished securing the materials that would be necessary for its completion, such as cedar (1 Kings 5:6) and stones (1 Kings 5:17) from Lebanon. Then the construction began. After many years of acquiring the necessary materials and executing the construction of the temple, the day came when it was finished. Solomon then moved to dedicate the temple, an event during which he sacrificed 22,000 oxen and 120,000 sheep (1 Kings 8:63). It was truly a momentous occasion for the people of Israel.

During the dedication of the temple, a spectacular event happened. After the Ark of the Covenant was placed in the Holy of Holies, God showed up to check the place out! As a result, the priests could no longer minister due to the manifestation of a cloud of God's glory. This cloud was known as the *shekinah* glory of God. The *shekinah* is defined as "the majestic presence or manifestation of God which has descended to 'dwell' among men."[49] Let us take a look at the account. It begins as the Ark of the Covenant was placed into the newly finished temple.

> And the priests brought the ark of the covenant of the Lord to its place in the Holy of Holies of the house, under the wings of the cherubim. For the cherubim spread forth their two wings over the place of the ark, and the cherubim covered the ark and its poles. The poles were so long that the ends of them were seen from the Holy Place before the Holy of Holies, but they were not seen outside; they are there to this day. There was nothing in the ark except the two tables of stone which Moses put there at Horeb, where the Lord made a covenant with the Israelites when they came out of the land of Egypt. **When the priests had come out of the Holy Place, the <u>cloud</u> filled the Lord's house, so the priests could not stand to minister because of the <u>cloud</u>, for the <u>glory of the Lord</u> had filled the Lord's house. Then Solomon said, The Lord said that He would dwell in the <u>thick darkness</u>.**
>
> (1 Kings 8:6–12 AMPC)

In the passage above I have underlined several key words that describe the *shekinah* glory of God. You will notice that the words <u>*cloud*</u>, and <u>*thick darkness*</u> are awfully familiar. These manifestations accompany God's entrance into our time-space because his entrance involves the use of an open portal. While this may sound incredible, the fact of the matter is that the manifestation of God's shekinah actually occurs via portal technology. The shekinah glory of God was the presence of God dwelling among men—through the use of a dimensional wormhole! Earlier in Israel's history, the shekinah manifested itself to Israel as the cloud by day and the pillar of fire by night (Exodus 13:21–22). It is incredible to think that the shekinah of God is—in effect—an open portal displaying God's manifest presence. As we read towards the end of the passage, Solomon quotes Scripture to reinforce the idea that God was visiting them because "the Lord said that he would dwell in the thick darkness."

From that day forward, as long as the shekinah was present in the temple, that building served as a dimensional portal to the third heaven. It was none other than the place where heaven and earth intersected. It was there that God's presence and atmosphere continually overlapped the earth. I can just imagine how amazing it must have been for the high priest who was allowed to enter this place once per year! And yet, whatever they may have experienced falls far short of an even greater work of God. This is the work of transforming you and me, and every other Christian, into a living, breathing temple for his Spirit.

PRESENT-DAY TEMPLES

"Know ye not that ye are the **temple** of God, and that the Spirit of God dwelleth in you?" (1 Corinthians 3:16).

In this passage, Paul was speaking to the Church at Corinth. He was informing them that Christians are the temple of God. This idea, as you may well imagine, was quite radical. To suggest that these people were the temple of God was to suggest that every function the temple was intended to have in this world was now taking place inside of each and every believer. While on the surface this may seem basic, particularly to those who have read the Bible several times, the magnitude of this revelation is actually quite extraordinary when placed in proper context.

The temple was a house in which God would manifest himself. When he would manifest it was called the shekinah glory. This would occur as God made an entrance through a dimensional portal for the purpose of dwelling amongst men. This would literally involve heaven and earth overlapping in that time-space. Therefore, what Paul is actually communicating is that in the same way that the temple functioned to achieve these things—so it is now with each and every Christian. We function as individual houses for the glory of God to dwell amongst men. Heaven and earth literally overlap upon the Christian's time-space when they allow their spiritual nature to overcome the flesh. Furthermore, heaven is permanently overlapped upon our spirits. Christians actually function as portals to the third heaven, meaning that we take heaven with us wherever we go. Take a look at some of these other verses detailing this incredible aspect of our faith.

"If any man defile the **temple** of God, him shall God destroy; for the **temple** of God is holy, which **temple** ye are" (1 Corinthians 3:17).

"What? know ye not that your body is the **temple** of the Holy Ghost which is in you, which ye have of God, and ye are not your own?" (1 Corinthians 6:19).

Again, as temples of God we are intended to function as portals between heaven and earth. In Paul's second letter to the Corinthian Church, he continues on to expound upon this aspect of their spiritual functionality (their functions occurring in higher dimensions). However, he takes it one step further. Paul goes on to explain that when Christians come together as the corporate Church, the conglomeration of their spiritual activity also functions as a temple for the shekinah glory of God. This is clearly communicated in the following verse, although it is not immediately apparent in the English language.

"And what agreement hath the temple of God with idols? for **ye** are the temple of the living God; as God hath said, I will dwell in them, and walk in them; and I will be their God, and they shall be my people" (2 Corinthians 6:16).

In this passage the word *ye* is translated from the Greek word *hymeis*. This word is an irregular plural form of the word *you*. As the verse continues, we see God being quoted as using the plural words *them*, *their*, and *they*. This passage is not directed at individual believers but at the corporate Church. While believers function as individual temples of the Living God, the corporate church is intended to fulfill the same functions. The difference is that the potential for displaying the true atmosphere of the presence and glory of God is ramped up by many orders of magnitude when Christians unite corporately. In other words, the ability to demonstrate his kingdom is greatly increased when people come together united on this agenda. As it is written:

"For wherever **two or three** are **gathered** (drawn together as My followers) in (into) My name, there I AM in the midst of them" (Matthew 18:20 AMPC).

The Bible goes on to discuss this aspect of the corporate Church's functionality in language that is so blindingly revelatory, this author can only scratch the surface as of this writing. Early in the Book of John, there is an incident when Jesus cleanses the physical temple by making a scourge of small cords and driving out the money changers with great aggression. Afterwards, his actions were questioned by the people. In responding to the Jews, he changed the definition of the temple from a physical construct to his very body. Of course he didn't tell them he was doing this, and as you can imagine, he left many people puzzled; but he certainly gave them something to think about!

"Then answered the Jews and said unto him, What sign shewest thou unto us, seeing that thou doest these things? Jesus answered and said unto them, Destroy this temple, and in three days I will raise it up. Then said the Jews, Forty and six years was this temple in building, and wilt thou rear it up in three days? **But he spake of the temple of his body**" (John 2:8–11).

In this passage, Jesus made it clear that his body was to be the new temple. However, the definition of "his body" isn't limited to the body that was resurrected on the third day. Spiritually, his body is actually comprised of the spirits of Christians. This is difficult to truly understand if we refuse to allow our comprehension to move beyond three-dimensional parameters. Please let go (if you haven't already) of how you've been trained to think things work. Just bear with me.

When our spirits are joined to the spirit of God (1 Corinthians 6:17), we become members of the body of Christ, which exists across the higher dimensions (spanning from the first heaven to the third heaven). This body ultimately finds its consummation where Jesus is seated in heavenly places (Ephesians 2:6) at the right hand of the Father (Acts 7:55, Psalm 110:1). Since we comprise his body and we are in his body, we are henceforth found "in him" (1 Corinthians 1:30, Philippians 3:9). Many verses that are very elusive to the new Christian gain much more clarity as our conscious mind begins to open up to spiritual principles. Straightforwardly stated, this means that we are beginning to understand reality in light of higher dimensions. The following passages give greater detail about our identity as the body of Christ.

"So **we, being many, are one body in Christ**, and every one members one of another" (Romans 12:5).

"For as the body is one, and hath many members, and all the members of that one body, being many, are one body: so also is Christ" (1 Corinthians 12:12).

"Now **ye are the body of Christ**, and members in particular" (1 Corinthians 12:27).

When the corporate Church comes together, it comes together as a temple that is actively being built. It is under construction, so to speak, and will be so until the Church corporately comes to the elusive "measure of the stature of the fullness of Christ" (Ephesians 4:13). The temple of God as a corporate spiritual structure is actually built out of the very spirits of those who have come to a saving knowledge of Jesus Christ. God does not use wood and stone to build his temple in the spirit realm. He actually uses the very spirits of Christians. If you were totally aware of what I have formerly defined as your unconscious mind, you would be able to clearly articulate what it is like to be used as "building material" (for lack of a better term) in the construction of the temple of God. This also is why we are referred to as living stones.

"You are built upon the foundation of the apostles and prophets with Christ Jesus Himself the chief Cornerstone. In Him the whole structure is joined (bound, welded) together harmoniously, and it continues to rise (grow, increase) into a holy temple in the Lord [a sanctuary dedicated, consecrated, and sacred to the presence of the Lord]. In Him [and in fellowship with one another] you yourselves also are being built up [into this structure] with the rest, to form a fixed abode (dwelling place) of God in (by, through) the Spirit" (Ephesians 2:20–22 AMPC).

"[Come] and, like **living stones**, be yourselves built [into] a spiritual house, for a holy (dedicated, consecrated) priesthood, to offer up [those] spiritual sacrifices [that are] acceptable and pleasing to God through Jesus Christ" (1 Peter 2:5 AMPC).

I want to take a step back at this juncture and place everything I have just stated into plain English. *Put simply, God uses human spirits as building material.* If you are thinking, "Well that is simple enough," I want to encourage you. *It is simple.* I literally went through all of those verses to make this simple point: God uses human spirits as building material.

In the corporate Church, God is using the spirits of Christians to build a spiritual temple for himself. The purpose is to manifest his shekinah glory to the world by using the Church to function as a portal between the first heaven and the third heaven. The same goes for individual believers. On a smaller scale, God designed individual believers to be used as a portal between the first heaven and the third heaven. *You were designed for the purpose of releasing heaven, the shekinah glory, and the unimaginable power of Jesus into every situation and circumstance touching your life.* Let us now take a look at how this can play out.

Peter's Shadow

In the Book of Acts, we read a story that simply boggles the carnal mind. We see the power of God's kingdom manifested through the ministry of the Apostle Peter. Before going further, let's take a look at what the passage has to say.

"And believers were the more added to the Lord, multitudes both of men and women. Insomuch that they brought forth the sick into the streets, and laid them on beds and couches, that at the least the shadow of Peter passing by might overshadow some of them. There came also a multitude out of the cities round about unto Jerusalem, bringing sick folks, and them which were vexed with unclean spirits: and they were healed every one" (Acts 5:14–16).

Many have read this account with a great deal of unbelief in their hearts. In their interpretation, they have approached the passage with the objective of distancing themselves from the text. The most common approach among certain groups within Christianity is to say, "Go Peter!" The idea of a "normal" Christian walking in such a degree of God's power that the sick are placed in the streets so that they can experience healing as the believer's mere shadow passes over them is borderline sacrilegious. The problem I find relative to this approach is that it is based out of a skewed paradigm. *It works to glorify who Peter was and not who Jesus is.* It was the power of Jesus that led to this activity, and Jesus is the same yesterday, today, and forever (Hebrews 13:8).

So, what actually happened here? What property of Peter's shadow allowed for such mighty manifestations of God's power? I submit to you that the shadow of Peter in this case served as an indicator of measurement. The measure of Peter's shadow was the measure of our time-space that was *characterized* by the Spirit of God within him. This would be similar to the way that the "Valley of the Shadow of Death" is a spiritual valley *characterized* by the measure of Death's shadow. Everything about the atmosphere of the valley over which Death's shadow abides reflects the *character* of Death and the realm over which he rules.

"Yea, though I walk through the **valley of the shadow of death**, I will fear no evil: for thou art with me; thy rod and thy staff they comfort me" (Psalm 23:4).

Likewise, the space occupied by the measure of Peter's shadow became characterized by the spiritual nature of Jesus and his kingdom.

This led to supernatural healing and deliverance in Peter's time-space. It revealed how the kingdom of God (or the realm in which God is King) is not meant to stay inside of our hearts but also to overlap our world. The kingdom of God is to be accessed by our spirit, rooted in our hearts, and released through our lives. This point is so very well-articulated in the Amplified Bible.

"Asked by the Pharisees when the kingdom of God would come, He replied to them by saying, The kingdom of God does not come with signs to be observed or with visible display, Nor will people say, Look! Here [it is]! or, See, [it is] there! For behold, **the kingdom of God is within you [in your hearts] and among you [surrounding you]**" (Luke 17:20–21 AMPC).

In closing out this chapter, let us highlight several key ideas. The kingdom of God is the realm in which God is King. It is within us, and it is intended to make its way out of us. When it does there is a demonstration of the power of God. There is also a manifestation of the will of God into real-time—changing the situations and circumstances present in our fallen world. As his "kingdom comes" we will watch the unveiling of the goals, agendas, and love of Jesus Christ. To this end, we have all been designed to operate as portals to the third heaven, thus, the reason that we are declared temples of the Spirit of God.

Furthermore, the body of Christ is designed to function as a temple corporately. We are built up into a spiritual temple as living stones, meaning that God actually uses human spirits to construct his spiritual temple. As a result, when we function according to our purpose, we operate as a corporate portal capable of exposing large portions of geography to the glory and majesty of God's realm. In light of this, to express the potential that God has in store for the corporate body of Christ is beyond communication. Yet, as the understanding of higher dimensions and all that they entail becomes better understood among believers, it is my firm conviction that the best is yet to come regarding the destiny of the body of Christ.

Epilogue

This book has been a joy to write. As the author, I have personally learned more than I could have bargained for. I have also been transformed. It is my prayer that this book has been a transformative experience for you as well. I want to take this opportunity to encourage you, the reader. If you made it this far I want to commend you. You have proven your desire to go beyond what many have falsely assumed is "all there is." There is no question that this book is deep. It was not written to be understood according to three-dimensional paradigms. Unfortunately, many of us begin our journey with God operating out of these very paradigms. Why wouldn't we? Therefore I want to encourage you to read this book a second time, and possible a third time.

This book is written in layers. As you read it the first time, you will only be able to benefit from what the Holy Spirit has revealed to you the first time through. The more you think about the truths in this book and mull over them, the more these things will unfold to your understanding. As they do, you will find your faith becoming stronger, and your perception of spiritual things expanding. The principle at work is that when it comes to spiritual things, it is the Holy Spirit that is your Teacher. My job is to present the information; the Holy Spirit's job is to teach you the information. He teaches you what you are ready for, and as you are ready for more, he will take you to the next level.

"But the Comforter (Counselor, Helper, Intercessor, Advocate, Strengthener, Standby), the Holy Spirit, Whom the Father will send in My name [in My place, to represent Me and act on My behalf], **He will teach you all things**. And He will cause you to recall (will remind you of, bring to your remembrance) everything I have told you" (John 14:26 AMPC).

Nonetheless, you may have reached this point and realized that you wouldn't have an answer if someone were to ask you, "What was the book about?" For those of you who fall into this category I will make it very simple. This entire book can actually be summed up in a very simple paragraph. Like all truth, it can be expanded almost infinitely, but it can also be broken down into its simplest form. Consider the following fraction: 4,936,290/5,923,548. While it looks like a big mess, it really reduces to a very simple truth. If both the top and bottom are divided by the number 987,258 we actually get the fraction: 5/6. They are two expressions of the same value, one is just significantly more complex. In like manner, this book can be summed up as follows:

This book discusses higher dimensions, parallel dimensions, and portals in light of biblical revelation. It discloses an in-depth assessment of the human condition according to biblical concepts. In doing this, the book sets up a paradigm out of which readers can begin to see their activities and God's activities in ways that transcend the physical plane. In addition, many elements of the kingdom of darkness are exposed in order to equip the reader with knowledge that will empower them to not be ignorant of the devil's schemes. In the end, the book establishes that Christians are intended to operate as gateways (or portals) between heaven and earth.

"Pray, therefore, like this: Our Father Who is in heaven, hallowed (kept holy) be Your name. **Your kingdom come, Your will be done on earth as it is in heaven**" (Matthew 6:9–10).

Visit the author at www.bridemovement.com!

Endnotes

1 Bullinger, E. W. *Number in Scripture; its supernatural design and spiritual significance.* Grand Rapids: Kregel Publications, 1967. Print.

2 "Dimension." Wikipedia. N.p., n.d. Web. 14 June 2012. <http://en.wikipedia.org/wiki/Dimensions

3 The question may arise that if Jesus has ascended above all heavens (Ephesians 4:10), why should we even try to conclude that he would be located in the third heaven (or paradise)? However, the Bible says of God that his throne is in heaven (Psalm 11:4, Psalm 103:19). There is an element of God that transcends all of the heavens, but his throne is still found in heaven. It is written that heaven is his throne and Earth his footstool (Isaiah 66:1). It is also written that he who swears by heaven swears by God's throne (Matthew 5:34, 23:22). The realm above all heavens is a mystery, but God remains accessible to redeemed men and elect angels upon his throne in the third heaven.

4 "dimension." *www.dictionary.com.* N.p., n.d. Web. 27 Sept. 2012. <dictionary.reference.com/browse/dimension?s=t>

5 "parallel." *www.dictionary.com.* N.p., n.d. Web. 27 Sept. 2012. <dictionary.reference.com/browse/parallel?s=t>

6 "perpendicular." *www.dictionary.com.* N.p., n.d. Web. 27 Sept. 2012. <dictionary.reference.com/browse/perpendicular?s=t>

7 "Further information - Category: how many cubes to do a hypercube?" *MateMatita.* N.p., n.d. Web. 15 Oct. 2012. <http://www.matematita.it/personali/index.php?blog=7&cat=153>

8 Ibid.

9 "Time." *Wikipedia.* Wikimedia Foundation, 27 Jan. 2014. Web. 27 Jan. 2014. <http://en.wikipedia.org/wiki/Time>

10 "Gravity." *Wikipedia.* Wikimedia Foundation, 27 Jan. 2014. Web. 27 Jan. 2014. <http://en.wikipedia.org/wiki/Gravity>

11 "Further information - Category: how many cubes to do a hypercube?" *MateMatita.* N.p., n.d. Web. 15 Oct. 2012. <http://www.matematita.it/personali/index.php?blog=7&cat=153>

12 Some may understand the subconscious as the "lower soul" or "lower self." It follows that the spirit is determined to be the "super conscious mind" or the "higher self." The soul is also called the "middle self." Reference. Harmon, Hugh, and Pamela Chilton. "WHY SUBCONSCIOUS PROGRAMMING AFFECTS YOU." *Odyssey of the Soul.* N.p., n.d. Web. 26 Aug. 2013. <http://www.odysseyofthesoul.org/freomm/programming.html>

13 Wolf, Fred Alan. "Shadows of Time, Space, Matter and Mind--A conclusion." *Time Loops and Space Twists: How God Created the Universe.* San Antonio, TX: Hierophant Publishing, 2013. 230. Print.

14 Wolf, Fred Alan. "'Til the Cows Come Home." *Time Loops and Space Twists: How God Created the Universe.* San Antonio, TX: Hierophant Publishing, 2013. 41–44. Print.

15 Ibid.

16 "Jewels Falling from Heaven in Puerto Rico « The Rising Light." *The Rising Light*. N.p., n.d. Web. 20 June 2012. <http://www.therisinglight. com/2009/jewels-falling-from-heaven-in-puerto-rico/>

17 "Gemstones From Heaven « The Rising Light." *The Rising Light*. N.p., n.d. Web. 20 June 2012. <http://www.therisinglight.com/category/ miracles/gemstones-from-heaven/>

18 "The Emerald Tablets of Thoth - Secret of Secrets." *Crystalinks Home Page*. N.p., n.d. Web. 27 Aug. 2013. <http://www.crystalinks.com/emer-ald15bw.html>

19 *Good News Bible: the Bible in Today's English version.* New York: American Bible Society, 1976. Print.

20 Ibid.

21 Charles, R. H. *Book of Enoch*. Eugene: Wipf & Stock Publishers, 2011. Print.

22 Some have given various reasons for concluding that Asael (or Azazel) is another name for Lucifer (aka Satan). One of the reasons is because references can be found using the name Lucifer to refer to, or to describe, Azazel. Azazel is also the Hebrew word translated *scapegoat* in Leviticus 16:8, 10, and 26. This can lead to the idea that Lucifer (in reference to Satan) and Azazel are the same entity. The truth is that names are often changed from one text to another as one works their way through literature referencing various angels and demons. This author (along with most commentators on the issue) does not see any justifica-tion for assuming these beings are the same entity. The clearest reason for this

conclusion is that while Azazel was judged and locked up along with those that rebelled in Genesis 6, Satan was left to roam the earth (Job 2:2).

23 Charles, R. H. *Book of Enoch*. Eugene: Wipf & Stock Publishers, 2011. Print.

24 Ibid.

25 I am aware that some have chosen to interpret the woman in this passage as the Church. Hippolytus, an early Church father, wrote the following in his work *Treatise on Christ and Antichrist*: 61. "By the 'woman then clothed with the sun,' he meant most manifestly the Church, endued with the Father's word, whose brightness is above the sun. And by 'the moon under her feet' he referred to her being adorned, like the moon, with heavenly glory. And the words, 'upon her head a crown of twelve stars,' refer to the twelve apostles by whom the Church was founded. And those, 'she, being with child, cries, travailing in birth, and pained to be delivered,' mean that the Church will not cease to bear from her heart the Word that is persecuted by the unbelieving in the world. 'And she brought forth,' he says, 'a man-child, who is to rule all the nations;' by which is meant that the Church, always bringing forth Christ, the perfect man-child of God, who is declared to be God and man, becomes the instructor of all the nations."

While I don't see a philosophical problem with this interpretation, some have taken this interpretation and stretched it to say that the man-child is a super-special company of last-day believers. Some even say that this man-child of super-special last-day believers will kick Satan out of heaven in the last days. I do not presently agree with this last point, and I feel that this requires a degree of conjecture. My main problem is that I do not know of any canon Scriptures that straightforwardly associate the Church with a "woman." The church is called a virgin (Matthew 25:2) and the wife of the Lamb (Ephesians 5:23, 27 and

Revelation 19:7). It is never called a "woman." Conversely, the nation of Israel is in fact called a "woman." Furthermore, the apostles are never straightforwardly associated with stars in canon Scripture. In contrast, we do have the dream of Joseph that fits the vision perfectly, explaining that the stars represent the twelve tribes of Israel. Therefore, I prefer to interpret the first verses of Revelation 12 in light of Joseph's dream. Interpreting this passage as I have done is clean and straightforward. It allows the Bible to interpret itself.

I will add that I do believe a group of leaders will arise in the church that will be extremely powerful in the last days. I would even go so far as to say it is possible that the Spirit of God could be breathing on this passage in order to point this fact out to certain people. Short of believers themselves being caused to kick Satan out of heaven, I do not find any philosophical problems with interpreting this passage in a similar way to Hippolytus. Some prophetic passages have layered fulfillments. For example, in the Book of Malachi, Elijah is prophesied to return before the day of the Lord. It is said that he will unite the fathers and the children (Malachi 4:5). Jesus explained that John the Baptist was Elijah who was prophesied to come (Matthew 11:14). Therefore, this prophecy was fulfilled. Yet I, along with many others, believe the Spirit of the Lord is breathing upon that passage in these days in a sort of secondary fulfillment. A work of the last days will involve uniting the older and younger generations (fathers and children). In like manner, I believe a secondary interpretation and fulfillment is possible with the passage in Revelation 12:1–6.

26 *The Sixth and Seventh Book of Moses*. Kila, MT: Kessinger Pub:1997. Print.

27 "Revelations of a Mother Goddess, researched and presented by David Icke, Interview with Arizona Wilder -- Transcript prepared by Tara Carreon at American Buddha Online Library." *The Ralph Nader Library*.

N.p., n.d. Web. 31 July 2012. <http://www.naderlibrary.com/icke.revela-
tionmothergoddess4.htm>

28 Interview with an Ex-Vampire. Dir. Michael Relfe. Perf. Bill Schnoebelen,
Stephanie Relfe. Mark 161718 Productions, 2005. DVD.

29 Hamlett, Carolyn. "Beyond the Physical Realm Blog." *Beyond the Physical
Realm Blog.* N.p., n.d. Web. 27 Aug. 2013. <http://www.beyondthephysicalrealm.
com>

30 Vine, W. E. *Vine's expository dictionary of Old & New Testament words.*
Nashville, Tenn.: T. Nelson Publishers, 2003. Print.

31 While many assume that this passage (Revelation 6:12–17) referencing the
sixth seal is a clear reference to the second coming of Jesus Christ, I strongly dis-
agree. It is true that verses 15—17 say, "And the kings of the earth, and the great
men, and the rich men, and the chief captains, and the mighty men, and every
bondman, and every free man, hid themselves in the dens and in the rocks of the
mountains; And said to the mountains and rocks, Fall on us, and hide us from
the face of him that sitteth on the throne, and from **the wrath of the Lamb**: For
the great day of his wrath is come; and who shall be able to stand?" However, as I
clearly outlined in my book *Noah's Ark and the End of Days* (Crane, MO: Official
Disclosure, 2010. 118—126. Print.), this conclusion is reached by <u>men</u>. This conclusion is drawn by people: humans that are fallen, easily deceived and fallible in
their conclusions. This fact becomes clear from the proper exegesis of the text. In
other words, this revelation is not given by God or an angel, but it is the response
of the earth dwellers to what is happening. The Apostle John is recording *their
conclusion* on the reason for this event taking place.

When we understand this, we can add to our interpretation the fact that the Bible records other places where people come to the wrong conclusion about something. For instance, in the Book of Job, Job's wife is recorded as saying he should curse God and die (Job 2:9). No one is going to build a doctrinal approach to God around this passage. This passage is there so we can see how people can come to the wrong conclusion. In the same way she came to the wrong conclusion, the people claiming the sixth seal is equivalent to the "wrath of the Lamb" arrive at the wrong conclusion. This is further evidenced by the fact that afterwards, when the seventh seal is opened, it leads to seven angels being given seven trumpets (Revelation 8:1–2).

This is important because Jesus is recorded as coming at the seventh or last trumpet (Revelation 11:15–18, 1 Corinthians 15:51–52, Revelation 10:7, 1 Thessalonians 4:16). This means all seven trumpets will have to sound after the sixth seal is opened. Furthermore, we will not see Jesus actually returning until the seventh trumpet is sounded. Due to a timeframe given to us by the fifth trumpet (five months, according to Revelation 9:5,10) it becomes impossible to say that at the sixth seal everything happens at once (the sixth seal = the seventh trumpet and everything in between).

While I assume the timeframe will be significantly longer between the sixth seal and the seventh trumpet than five months, this evidence proves, without any room for argument, that a minimum of five months must separate the sixth seal and the seventh trumpet. They are not the same event, nor can the sixth seal be chalked up to a "secret rapture," as the context is clearly destructive and world-shaking in nature. No one is wondering why people vanished; people are trying to hide! Is Jesus coming to destroy twice? No. The most logical conclusion is to understand that the sixth seal is a counterfeit second coming being executed by the kingdom of darkness. It will present the antichrist to the world in a way that fools the world into thinking Jesus has actually returned. After this, the trumpet judgments will begin to sound.

32 *New American Standard Bible*. Reference ed. Chicago: Moody Press, 1977. Print.

33 Adams, Mike, and the Health Ranger Editor of NaturalNews.com (See all articles...). "A real Planet of the Apes? UK scientists secretly grew human-animal hybrids in laboratory experiments." *Natural health news*. N.p., n.d. Web. 2 July 2012. <http://www.naturalnews.com/033100_human-animal_hybrids_Planet_of_the_Apes.html>

34 Ferrell, Ana. *Regions of Captivity: One of the Most Powerful Ways to be Delivered*. Shippensburg: Destiny Image Publishers, 2010. 110-111. Print.

35 Brown, Rebecca. "Discipline Within the Brotherhood." *He came to set the captives free*. New Kensington, PA: Whitaker House, 1997. 64-65. Print.

36 "GADARA - JewishEncyclopedia.com." *JewishEncyclopedia.com*. N.p., n.d. Web. 31 Oct. 2012. <http://www.jewishencyclopedia.com/articles/6457-gadara>

37 "JERASH - A BRIEF HISTORY." *Al Mashriq - the Levant - Lebanon and the Middle East - BÃ¸rre Ludvigsen*. N.p., n.d. Web. 31 Oct. 2012. <http://almashriq.hiof.no/jordan/900/930/jerash/jerash.html>

38 "All About Umm-Qays." *Umm-Qays Web Site*. N.p., n.d. Web. 31 Oct. 2012. <http://umm-qays.itgo.com/all.html>

39 Gesenius, Wilhelm; Robinson, Edward (trans.) (1844). *A Hebrew and English lexicon of the Old Testament: including the Biblical Chaldee*. Boston, MA: Crocker & Brewster. p. 976.

40 Simon, Maurice (trans.); Slotik, Israel W. (trans.) (1935). "Folio 74b". In Epstein, Isidore. *Baba Bathra: chapters I - VI; translated into English with notes, glossary and indices.* London, England: Soncino Press.

41 Conybeare, F.C., and Joseph Peterson. "The Testament of Solomon." Twilit Grotto Esoteric Archives. 1997. Accessed October 20, 2015. http://www.esotericarchives.com/solomon/testamen.htm.

42 Ibid.

43 "Portal." *Dictionary.com.* N.p., n.d. Web. 4 Nov. 2012. <http://dictionary.reference.com/browse/portal?s=t>

44 "Wormhole." *Dictionary.com.* N.p., n.d. Web. 4 Nov. 2012. <http://dictionary.reference.com/browse/wormhole?s=t>

45 "Space-time." *Dictionary.com.* N.p., n.d. Web. 4 Nov. 2012. <http://dictionary.reference.com/browse/wormhole?s=t>

46 "Book of Jasher 9." *Christian Classics Ethereal Library.* N.p., n.d. Web. 8 Nov. 2012. <http://www.ccel.org/a/anonymous/jasher/9.htm>

47 "Ziggurat." *Dictionary.com.* N.p., n.d. Web. 18 Nov. 2012. <http://dictionary.reference.com/browse/ziggurat?s=t>

48 Black, Gods, Demons and Symbols, s.v. "Temples and Temple Architecture," p. 175.

49 "SHEKINAH - JewishEncyclopedia.com." *JewishEncyclopedia.com.* N.p., n.d. Web. 18 Nov. 2012. <http://www.jewishencyclopedia.com/articles/13537-shekinah>